To - Dad
Father's D[...]
June 19/[...]

Love from,
Vivian

Christmas 2001
Dear Melody:
I thought you
might enjoy this.
Mabel Breen was
a cousin of my
father. Love J.

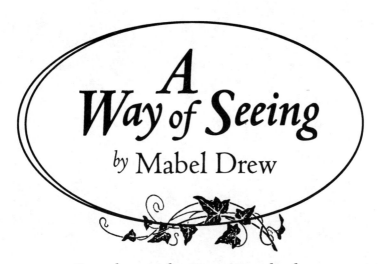

A Way of Seeing

by Mabel Drew

Introduction by Roger Bainbridge

QUARRY PRESS

Canadian Cataloguing in Publication Data

Drew, Mabel
    A way of seeing
ISBN 1-55082-096-6

    I. Title.
PS3554.R79W39 1993   081   C93-090521-0

Design by Susan Hannah.
Cover art by Dorothy Renals, reproduced by permission of the artist.
Typeset by Quarry Press, Inc.
Printed and bound in Canada
by Webcom Limited, Toronto, Ontario.

Published by Quarry Press, Inc.,
P.O. Box 1061, Kingston, Ontario K7L 4Y5.

CONTENTS

for Lorna and Linda,
Christopher and Alicia

PREFACE

Each of us has our own way of looking at life; the past and the present appearing as shaped by personal experience and colored by genetic preferences that may have been formed centuries ago.

These essays offer the reader my way of seeing; different in detail to yours but you will relate to it at many points. Most of them deal with nostalgia for I have a habit of looking backwards more often than ahead. Even when very young I was preoccupied with the past for childhood seemed to me to be, not blissful and perfect, but magic and precious; a treasure to hold on to and cherish for all time. I envied Peter Pan, not understanding then what a sad little boy he was.

If I appear in my writing to be making an effort to escape the horrors of today's world, it isn't that I deliberately turn my back. It's only that we all need a little respite at times. It isn't wrong to turn around for a moment and look into the sunrise, even to laugh a little. We simply rest for awhile and renew our strength.

It's been a good life for me on the whole. There's nature and books and people, and that misty green hollow in the woods where the violets grow. "The world is so full of a number of things."

INTRODUCTION

A mission statement in the first issue of *The Whig-Standard Magazine* promised that the publication would be a special place for quiet voices carefully protected from "the daily clamor of urgent headlines." None of the quiet voices indigenous to *The Magazine* and its successor, *The Companion*, has been more special to us and to our readers than that of Mabel Drew. Her enchanting columns, which helped to shape the personality of *The Magazine* from the start, betray her keen awareness of the natural world, her uncommon understanding of human behavior, and her passion for the written word.

She writes with equal wisdom about the seasons of the year and the seasons of life. She is both teacher and student, and all of life is her textbook. It is the minutiae of nature that most often arrest her inquisitive eye: "I like small: microcosms that suggest infinity but don't boggle the mind with gargantuan forms and distances. . . . I love nooks and crannies; the way a small clump of brittle reeds lays its silhouette on the sand where one can mark a water beetle's track through the dappled shadow."

Like a child, she "stands agog" at the "magic of the incredible facts of nature." In one column she marvels at the capacity for affection in an animal as huge as an elephant or as nasty as a crocodile; she is enchanted by the loving care they lavish upon their young: "I'm an anthropomorphic old girl, and this incidence of tenderness among nature's wild creatures devastates me so that I go all soft inside like a warm chocolate nougat. If love in the wild is nothing more than a beguiling ruse to trick all life into reproducing its kind, then so be it. It's a lovely ruse. But I'll bet you a dollar to a dolphin it's more than that."

She may write about a jazz band in New Orleans, a maple sugar shack in Vermont, the many ways of eating an ice cream cone, or the intricate behavior of spiders. Frequently she delves into the precious realm of childhood memories: "My earliest daydream was that I could survive like some wild forest creature on roots and berries, sleep like a young rabbit in a thicket and become friends with the fairy population in whom I thoroughly believed."

Her column is a repository for gentle thoughts and positive experiences. In a world a-jangle with daily news of human suffering, the reassuring voice of Mabel Drew is welcome.

ROGER BAINBRIDGE

Reflections
in a Child's Eye

THE CHILD IN THE WOOD

I met a little girl at the end of the road where the wood begins and we walked together under the trees. The ground slopes down there to a marshy place where the earth is dark and wet and the branches close in above, making a kind of secret retreat. She walked beside me quietly, looking up and smiling almost as though she had been waiting for me.

There's a fat, fallen bough of an old tree that lies across the wild grasses making a natural bench for us to sit on. She sat with her knees drawn up, clasping them in her arms and looking into the undergrowth as though remembering something. "This is where I come for the first violets," she said, nodding toward an area lush with sweet fern and the creeping foliage of myrtle.

"I know," I said. "I find them here too."

"When I was a little girl," I began, for somehow I felt I could talk to her, that she was receptive and sympathetic, and her eyes, blue as corn-flowers, encouraged me with a gentle expectancy. "There was a hill where I used to go that was blue with long-stemmed violets in the spring. It seems odd for violets to be growing that way, out in the sunlight on a hillside. Did you ever see them like that, away from the trees?"

She nodded, with a smile that was infinitely wise. "I've seen them," she said.

We sat in silence for a while. It all seemed so right and natural that we should be together here in this hidden corner of the woods. We weren't far from the highway but we heard no traffic sounds, only the random rustling of leaves and a lone bird crying a solitary note. Presently the child stood up and walked away from me a few steps. She paused, and as I waited to see what she would do I realized that she was singing — very softly — scarcely audible. But the tune sounded famil-iar. "Sing a little louder," I urged. "I think I know that song."

So she began again raising her voice a trifle so I could hear. And the words that she sang were:

I know a place where the sun is like gold
And the cherry blooms burst with snow.
And down underneath is the loveliest nook
Where the four-leaf clovers grow....

I was so delightfully surprised that I interrupted her. "Oh, I love that song. I haven't heard it for so long!"

She laughed as though she were as pleased as I. "And this one," she said. "It's a different kind of song, a fun song." And she sang again, smiling into my eyes all the while.

Oh where, oh where has my little dog gone?
Oh where, oh where can he be?
With his tail cut short and his ears cut long,
Oh, where, oh where can he be?

She ran to me then and gave me a quick hug. "I know! I know!" I laughed with her but there were tears behind my eyes. "My mother sang that to me and she always had such a teasing look when she sang it as though it were a kind of sly surprise," I said. And I looked at the little girl again, searchingly, feeling the strangeness of this encounter and our inexplicable rapport. It was lovely and it was eerie. I enquired where she had learned the song.

"My mother too," she whispered, in a way that sounded oddly conspiratorial.

I felt that I wanted to test her though I had no idea what it was I wanted to confirm. "Did you ever pretend," I asked, with some embarrassment, "when you were in a place like this, I mean, all by yourself in the woods or in some wild place, that the trees had souls, that they had some comprehension of themselves, of me — and, and...." I couldn't go on for she stood waiting with that innocent, inscrutable gaze while this disconcerted adult stuttered before her like a fool. She put her hand on mine. "Of course," she assured me quietly. "I know. I know all about it. I even hug the trees sometimes."

I turned away because I felt the tears on my cheeks and I didn't want her to see. Without looking at her I could see so clearly the blue eyes, the curly hair, blond as mine had been so very long ago. For a long moment I stood within her aura wondering what magic it was that held me.

13

And then I felt cold and I knew that she had gone. When I turned I saw her at the edge of the copse and there was a mist there and, beyond the mist, a sort of pale violet shadow that stretched into the distance. I wanted to call her to stay. She turned as though she had heard my unspoken words, raised her hand in a slow gesture of farewell. Then the mist closed around her and she was gone.

THE LADIES OF PEACH TREE STREET

How mother became acquainted with the ladies of Peach Tree Street I don't know. They were wealthy, middle-aged spinsters when I knew them, members of prominent Philadelphia families. To me they were Miss Logan and Dr. Evelyn, and somehow they had taken a liking to me. Thus it came about that I spent the occasional weekend with them and was treated now and then to performances at the Academy of Music and the Shubert-Keith Theatre.

Miss Logan had a big square face with a sudden smile that turned on easily, and I sensed her real affection for me. But I was a little afraid of Dr. Evelyn. She was abrupt at times, particularly if I walked into a room where she was in conversation with someone. Dr. Evelyn monopolized any guests, maneuvering them into corners, where they sat looking trapped and nervous. On one occasion I intruded when she was talking with a German professor who actually had, on one cheek, a sword scar suffered in a duel. The doctor's red face grew redder as she glared at me and told me to amuse myself elsewhere. So I went into the library and found a plain-cover copy of *Lady Chatterley's Lover*, which effectively amused this 11-year old for an hour or more. The doctor had bought it in Europe at the time when it was "banned in Boston."

The Peach Tree address was the couple's city residence. They also owned an old inn out Paoli way — Philadelphia's Main Line area — which they'd restored on the outside to its original colonial design and renovated inside to their convenience. Stump Tavern they called it, because of the lovely fat tree-stump that stood on the front lawn. I fell in love with that stump and would sit crosslegged on it gazing at that charming residence and pretending that I was the poor little rich girl who lived there.

There was a cunning small wood on the edge of the property and in the middle of it a clearing with a flat stone for dreaming and a hollow tree-trunk lying among tangled grasses and berry bushes. Here I played with imaginary playmates or read some book much too old for me from the library shelves. One day a rabbit disappeared into the hollow log, but though I sat as still as a stick for a long time, I never saw it come out again.

In the fall when the air nipped at our noses and leaves surged red and gold and tawny, we took walks down country lanes. Home again, we drank hot chocolate out of thick mugs, served by Hulda in starched white apron, while Hulda's daughter Tina, fragile and fair as a fairy, peeped shyly around the corner of the door until invited in.

Of the two homes I liked Stump Tavern best, but the Peach Tree house intrigued me. It was one in a row on a cobbled street something like the famous Elfreth's Alley, where Benjamin Franklin, walking along eating a bun for his lunch, first saw the woman who would become his wife. Peach Tree was a short, narrow way, a dark, secret lane of a street hidden in the unsavory neighborhood of Market, Race and Vine. Here too the house's exterior had been restored to its original facade. What fascinated me most while visiting there was Manuel, the Filipino house-boy. In his white jacket with high neckband and soft slippers he shuffled about his duties, one of which was to serve at table. In my desire to impress Manuel with my familiarity with gracious living, I was self-conscious and clumsy as he stood beside me, extending a silver tray from which I was to serve myself. I fancied I saw a glint of amusement in his soft brown eyes and sensed that even this servant was a more sophisticated individual than I. However, before the meal was over, it became obvious that neither amusement nor sophistication were responsible for Manuel's expression. He had been into the cooking sherry.

My Stump Tavern and Peach Tree weekends were glimpses into a privileged world that I fantasized about but never hoped to attain. They were stimulating, enlightening intervals that I treasured — but that were perhaps not always good for me. Sometimes there were days after my return home when I felt dissatisfied with my own circumstances and unreasonably critical. My behavior after one memorable homecoming must have been a sore trial to my family. That was when the Stump Tavern proprietors found it inconvenient to drive me home and called upon a friend to do so. That friend was Mrs. Gordon McGooch, wealthy matron and noted Philadelphia philanthropist. Her long black limousine drew up before the little brick house on Baynton St., the liveried chauffeur sprang to open the door, and out stepped *me*, darting my glance along the neighbors' windows for awed spectators. I took a lot of humbling after that. But now I know I wouldn't have changed my own remembered childhood world for any other.

THE BUTTON BOX

The button box sat on a shelf in the hall closet beside a battered rag clown named Charlie. Other closet residents were our winter clothes and several articles of old-fashioned women's wear in which my sister and I used to play "dress up." So attired, we climbed to the top of the chest of drawers and pretended we were riding, grandly, in a horse-drawn carriage.

The buttons were like toys to me. Sitting on the front bedroom floor under the pale glow of the gas lamp while Mother worked away at the old White treadle sewing machine, I arranged them into all sorts of designs. The sparkle of the glass ones set off by the shimmering light delighted me. I've always loved sparkle. The shining black buttons called "jets" were my favorites, though I know now they were simply black glass. Real jet buttons were expensive; a type made popular in Victoria's England by the bereaved queen, who wore them on her black mourning costumes from the time her beloved Albert died until her own death in 1901. Among prescribed rules of etiquette for the mourning period of the time was the injunction that "all pins, buckles, etc. must be of jet."

I liked to set the smaller buttons — usually pearl types or colored agate that Mother could buy for two cents a dozen — in a row, to serve as students in a classroom. At the head, the "teacher," or large black horn disk with which I identified, put them through their lessons of poetry recitations and songs. Many years later it amused me to see my own little girls playing at identical "pretends" without any suggestions from me; in fact, one of them used to conduct the same classroom scene with creamed peas on toast.

At the time I knew only that the buttons in Mother's button box were fascinating, pretty trinkets that afforded me hours of quiet pleasure. Now I know something about their composition: the pearl (shell) buttons, "very stylish for white waists"; the mother-of-pearl cat's eye ball button, handsome and dressy, for which one paid as much as fifteen cents the dozen. If Mother ordered such merchandise from the Sears & Roebuck catalog she had to add two cents extra for postage.

Today, as I stand in line at the post-office wicket waiting to mail a parcel, and to learn how many dollars it will cost, I brood on this matter.

My own button box dates back forty-five years and holds a motley assortment at which collectors would turn up their noses. There are no milk or camphor glass specimens from the 19th century with painted flower or animal designs; no French molded horn types inlaid with silver; not even a small brass picture button such as lined a Victorian lady's tight-fitting bodice to the count of seventeen. I do have a set of brass sleeve buttons from a First World War army uniform that Aunt Edith Day sewed on to a doll's corduroy jacket she made for her own children many years ago. Button collections like mine grow from the popular conviction that "this may come in handy some day." Now there they lie, like multi-colored pebbles in a stream, waiting for the day when they will be of use again.

Why do I keep them? Mostly for nostalgic reasons, I guess. There are a few from a set of kelly-green plastics that climbed all the way up one side of the first dress I ever made, when Singer's store on Princess St. gave a series of sewing lessons. Several little gold self-shank buttons once adorned matching blue and lilac velvet dresses made for my little daughters by the late Mrs. Harry Cook, a superb dressmaker and my good friend. I don't remember that large reddish one that looks like a thin slice of salami. But here is the red set from the red pajamas I made to wear in the hospital when I had my gall bladder out. Lovely memories!

Some of these days I'm going to throw them all out. Just like I'm going to throw out all those old manuscripts and carbon copies of stuff I've been writing for forty-five years, now bursting the seams of an enormous old broken-down black suitcase. Meanwhile, I'll set them back in the hall closet, as my mother did before me, to rest beside some winter clothes, a couple of my old out-of-style dresses that I can't make up my mind to get rid of, and a torn stuffed replica of Beatrix Potter's Mrs. Tiggywinkle, instead of the rag clown of my childhood.

THE FRONT STEPS

We sit there on hot summer afternoons when heat shimmers like molten glass above the dusty pavement. Bees bumble about Mother's one rose bush in a corner of the pocket-handkerchief yard. Though dry and anemic-looking, the bleeding-heart never stops bleeding, however high the temperature soars. I've seen it blooming in blazing July in a bed of cinders by the railroad track.

They are wide stone steps, nice to sit on, especially when the gentle shadow of the house lies upon them. Ours is one of a row of five brick houses, separated and fronted by black wrought-iron fences, each with its own tidy green lawn. Ours is the only one with a rose bush, and Mother is proud of it. It *has* to bloom luxuriantly, because she prays that it will. You can't beat God for growing roses.

We sit there on a summer evening while a little breeze riffles through the leaves of the tree of heaven that grows through the sidewalk. Sometimes we have a quarter from Mother, and her cut-glass fruit bowl, to go to Samuels' drug store for ice-cream. We come home with the bowl full to overflowing with scoops of vanilla, chocolate and strawberry flavors, all for twenty-five cents. That, with a bottle of homemade root beer fetched from the basement, is heavenly fare. Fifty years later the more sophisticated palate will still think so.

In the playground across the street tall black boys play basketball. It is an integrated playground, but the young people don't integrate. The color of the game depends on who gets there first, black or white. The later ones wait their turn. All except the children on the slides and swings, who know playing together is fun whatever color you are.

I sit on the steps waiting for Mother to come home from the avenue with her bulging string bag. It is a wonder to us what an amount that string bag holds. The syncopated tinkle of a player piano comes through Mrs. Ornstein's open parlor windows, soft-pedalled, unintrusive on the lazy mood of the warm afternoon. "I can't give you anything but love, baby." That's all right. That's a-plenty, in this long, languorous moment of eternity. Through the fence rails slithers the Nelson's orange cat,

Timmy (the one Mother calls Timothy-Titus-Philemon), and disappears into the alleyway. A sparrow shivers ecstatically having a dust bath in the middle of the street, while another pecks at a pat of dried manure from the milkman's horse. Like Keats with his nightingale, "A drowsy numbness pains my sense." Life can go on this way forever and ever for all I care.

I sit on the steps waiting for the postman. Barely into my teens, I am about to be discovered by the editor of McCall's magazine, whose delighted acceptance will arrive any day now. With a nod and a cool smile the man in the blue serge uniform walks by, and my mind throws a bad word after him, quickly followed by a heavenward request for forgiveness. There's always tomorrow, I assure myself tearfully, and try to settle down to a calm wait. (I wait twenty-one years. But it finally comes. And several more.)

Unlike the Pennsylvania Dutch out Lancaster way, we don't scrub our front steps every morning. Only sometimes we toss a pail of water over them and slosh it about with a broom. All of us keep our fences bright with black paint. I like to see them after a shower, when they glow with a high gloss, drops of rain suspended like crystal beads. The sun bursts out, and the garden spider's web between the roses and the brick house wall suddenly shines and shimmers with silver drops.

I sit on the steps watching the silent parade go by, tense with curiosity, wondering what will happen next; fearful that it may demand my participation; drawing back against the immutable stone, yet increasingly excited — because I know my turn will come.

Prolonging this tranquil hour, I sit on the steps.

A FLOCK OF SEVEN

Five birds moved across the middle distance of the evening sky on their way to some sunset resting place, and Ruthie Jenkins, raising her eyes at that moment, spoke the traditional magic words: "Flock of birds, flock of birds, may I have my wish." This was the opportunity I was waiting for. I had decided that I was going to be a part of myth-making, contributing to the rules if not creating a new one. "That doesn't count," I told Ruthie. "It's not a flock unless there are seven." I waited to see if my rule of seven would catch on among my schoolmates. It did. It wasn't long before it came back to me: "It takes seven to make a flock."

So the lore of childhood grows, though not always in so calculated a manner. In transmission the wording is altered, regional dialects affect pronunciation, changing one word into another, giving new meaning to the expression or creating a chant of rhythmic gibberish. While reading that fascinating study of the rhymes and chants and play patter of pre-teenagers *The Love and Language of Schoolchildren*, by Iona and Peter Opie, I was reminded of those sayings popular among my own peers when I was in grammar school. Lines that I had assumed were exclusively ours, spontaneous on the lips of a friend greeting the first star in an evening sky of smokey sapphire, were chanted, contextually, centuries ago:

Star light, star bright,
First star I've seen tonight,
I wish I may, I wish I might,
Have the wish I wish tonight.

We tried to be the first to shout, "Yakkie on the funnies," when *The Philadelphia Evening Bulletin* arrived each day. Which meant, obviously, that we wanted to be the first to open the paper on the floor and lie propped on our elbows to read the adventures of Winnie Winkle or Ben Webster and his dog Briar. The nearest word I can find to *yakkie* refers to Yak Bob Day, an English county expression for Royal Oak Day, having nothing to do with "firsties," as we used it. However, there were other ways of declaring first rights. *"Bags I"* was popular, and still is, in parts of England; while a small boy, eager for a game of marbles, might shout, "Iddy, iddy onker; my first conker." Naturally, if you were lucky enough to be named "Eenie" in the "eenie-meenie-miney-mo" count down, you would be first on your "onesies" in the bouncing ball game of Alarie.

I have always thought that a certain nonsensical rhyme was invented by my brother Larry. Only now do I learn that it's at least a century old. With slight changes from the earlier verse, our version is: "Julius Caesar, the great Roman geezer, / Got hit in the beezer with a lemon squeezer." Another verse we had, speaking in turn, is by no means modern. Veering slightly from the original, one began: "What's your name? — Puddin' and Tame. — What's your number? — Cucumber."

When my friend and I spoke a word simultaneously, without preamble we linked little fingers and, looking into the sky as though a passing cloud bore some clue, went through a performance that is international, with regional differences: "Bread. — Butter. — What goes up the chimney? — Smoke. Blue, Blue, make my wish come true. — White, white, make my wish come right. — I will not speak until I'm spoken to." Should we break the rule and speak first, our wish would go ungranted.

Hilarious to us children was the contradictory phrase. We would chant gleefully a verse that began, "One fine day in the middle of the night / Two dead men got up to fight." This is reminiscent of Carroll with his ". . . the sun was shining with all its might. / And this was odd because it was the middle of the night." But the contradictory line is older than Carroll, and we have some examples of it from 18th-century texts. Proudly, as though we had composed the parody ourselves, we would sing out, "I went to the pictures tomorrow. / I took a front seat in the back." What could be more inanely delightful than our version of Whittier's poem that began, "Blessings on thee, little man, / Barefoot boy with shoes of tan" or similarly: "The barefoot boy with shoes on / Stood sitting on the grass."

Unconsciously children preserve history, borrow from other cultures and reflect their own. They commemorate events, tragic or happy or scandalous; it all comes out as fun and games in the jargon of the schoolyard. It's a merry and secret linguistic world that pokes fun at life and holds back the dark for a while. All too soon they recognize the shadows for what they are.

CLOUD PICTURES

The little girls of that 1927 summer sat cross-legged on the grass under the young maples. The windless air held the afternoon in a timeless embrace and sunlight lay upon it like soft silk. They sat holding their dolls; dolls with china heads and cloth bodies, while between them on a lace doily the pieces of a toy tea set had been carefully laid.

These little girls may not have been all "sugar and spice, and everything nice" as the song goes, but in their best clothes on a sunny afternoon they had the appearance. Their shoes were of shiny black patent-leather with a strap buttoned over white silk knee socks. Their dresses were of dimity and dotted swiss and one had a bertha collar. Long blond curls hung over one's shoulders while the brunette wore bangs with side hair pinned back with gay barrettes. They sat talking quietly as they supposed young mothers would talk, interrupting themselves at times to admonish their babies to "sit still and behave."

They called each other "Mrs." and commented on the weather and the ailments of their children. Politics they were not well enough informed to discuss but they did know some of the more exciting current events, especially the flight of Charles Lindbergh in his monoplane *Spirit of St. Louis*. The tall, lean, shy aviator and his lonely sky journey across the Atlantic had captured their imaginations, as it had that of the whole world. This event had made them acutely airplane-conscious so that now, when they heard the small sustained thunder of a distant aircraft, they jumped to their feet, dropping their long-suffering children onto their heads and scattering tea cups about the grass. "There it is!" they cried, pointing excitedly. "See. Here it comes." "I wonder if it's Lindy." "Hey! Maybe it *is* Lindy. Maybe he can see us. Let's wave." And they stood there looking up into the blue heavens, waving frantically at the silver speck that grew and growled over their heads, then dwindled off into silence and space.

They scuffed back to their places under the tree, snatched up their dolls and scolded them for making such a shambles of the tea set. But it was impossible to settle down to a docile tea party after the excitement of the airplane. After considerable discussion they decided what they wanted to do most was to go the corner store and buy a bag of candy, providing their mothers would come through with a nickel. For any more than that they hardly dared hope, nor did they require it for an ample treat.

Skipping down the sidewalk to the "confectionery" they speculated on what "penny candy" they would buy. Such a variety lay behind the glass case awaiting their selection. Licorice whips gave you a lot for your money. On the other hand, sometimes a cinnamon potato had a penny hidden in it. There might be as many as a dozen kernels of candy corn for one cent. Or three chewy spearmint leaves. There were marshmallow bananas, sugar-coated licorice "nigger babies," and tootsie rolls. A grab bag held an assortment of sour balls, nonpareils, colored rock candy and gum drops. A nickel's worth of penny candy would keep their jaws working for hours.

Chewing slowly and ecstatically they made their way home over the hot pavement. "I wonder what the clouds look like to Lindy," said the curly-haired one through a lump of marshmallow banana. The brunette, munching away on a tootsie roll, wondered if it would be like flying through whipped cream. "Wouldn't it be great to have your mouth and eyes and ears all full of whipped cream?" They giggled and sputtered and wiped their mouths with the backs of their hands to keep from staining their crisp, clean frocks. Soon they were back on the soft, green lawn, still chewing their sweets, pointing out to each other cloud pictures in the afternoon sky.

Somewhere now, and forever, held in the mysterious embrace of Time, two little girls sit cross-legged under the young maple trees. The sun lays upon them like soft silk. Their talk is like the drone of drowsy bees while memory holds the door for the wistful old.

WISTER WOODS

On the corner stood the Brethwaite mansion, and that was where I turned to go to Wister Woods. There the black gardener displayed all his gleaming white teeth as he reminded me to stop on my way home while he picked me a bouquet of peonies. It wasn't a mansion really, but we called it that, seeing it from the steps of the little brick house down Baynton Street, the intriguing turrets, the bay windows and lovely old trees making circles of shade on soft grass.

Not far past Brethwaite's I turned on to a path so dark with overhanging foliage that with one step one could suddenly vanish from sight. To my right were the back gardens of Rubicam Avenue, long and narrow and bound by wrought-iron fences. Tom Daly, dialect poet of Little Italy, lived here. Later on my brother Cecil bought one of those gracious Victorian homes. His garden gate opened on to a park area and a tennis court, where he often played.

At the end of the tennis court, where I could sit and see without being seen, was a stand of Lombardy poplars and, right in the center where you'd never suspect it, a fountain, where a little boy sat on a frog from whose stone mouth gushed forth a bright stream. Generally the court was deserted when I wandered there, and often I lay on the grass looking into the sky through a pattern of leaves. No one bothered me in that peaceful place. Now, in these troubled times, a child could not be safely there alone.

There was another entrance to the woods. I had a choice. Sometimes I borrowed the druggist's dog, Tek, named after a brand of toothbrush. And then I'd go in off Shedaker Street over an equally hidden path that seemed rather sinister to me. There was a dark hollow there which, when explored, revealed patches of irascible nettles and broadleaved, acrid-smelling plants. And oozing through, too turgid to flow, lay a band of black water like the river of death. Good things couldn't happen there, and once my curiosity was satisfied, I walked past quickly and tried to think of happier places.

Places like the Indian Rock, a great, pocketed rock on the east side of the woods jutting out of a hill. I could be monarch of all I surveyed there, standing on the crest and looking out over Belfield Avenue, or I could crawl into a miniature cave and play at being one of nature's smaller wild creatures. I'm not sure why it was called Indian Rock, but I assumed it had some association with the Leni-Lenapes, a tribe of Indians of the Delaware. We had picnics there, sitting in hollows and on ledges, eating bologna and cheese sandwiches made with bread we had to slice ourselves and homemade root beer still cool from the refrigerator.

Across the avenue the woods continued beyond a field where I picked burnished golden buttercups. There were daisies and Queen Anne's lace and butter-end-eggs and all those meadow flowers. The star-of-Bethlehem shone along the roadside, but I passed it by, for I soon learned that, once picked, it faded quickly like sky stars at sunrise. Although we loved bouquets, my sister made a poster with the legend "Let's enjoy, not destroy, the wild flowers," and we tacked it on the bedroom wall beside the framed motto "Thou, God, seest me." I thought it so clever of Helen and didn't know until years later that her injunction wasn't original.

Then we came to the sweet shade of the woods again, the beeches and oaks and a little grotto where a pure stream fell out of the rock and people came for miles to fill their water pails and bottles; city people who weren't as fortunate as I, who could be hidden among the trees of Wister Woods within five minutes of leaving my front door. When a small volcano of rage seethed within and I daren't explode at home, I ran to Wister, where the hot lava could erupt harmlessly. I read poetry there, leaning against a tree trunk, and if I was very still, and lucky, a rabbit might come close enough that I could watch its nose twitch over a green lunch. By some miracle Wister Woods remain much the same as they were in my childhood, inviting other little girls to wander about and play their make-believe games. But I doubt that they do. There are predatory beasts in Wister Woods these days who eat little girls.

SECRET TREASURES OF THE HEART

She knew where the yellow primrose grew and the ox-eyed daisies. And she had marked the slope where quaker ladies, discreet as their namesakes, bloomed unobtrusively, low against the ground. It seemed right that these treasures should remain hidden in her heart, unshared secrets for her own quiet contemplation. There were other wayside and meadow flowers she shared and enjoyed sharing, but these she held back. The wisdom of childhood told her that one must always withhold a portion of oneself; that to tell all is to lose a part of that substance that made her herself and no other. Her secrets were precious. She savored them.

The wild flowers of summer were a constant pleasure. They were not merely passive parts of the scenery to be noted and admired in passing. They had their stories and their uses. Dandelions now; one split the stems and they curled gracefully like the loops of her hair-ribbon bow. The blossom grew old, the golden head went white and wispy like her grandmother's hair. Then you blew the delicate strands away into the air; blew until they were all gone. You could tell the time by the number of puffs it took to blow all the fluff away.

The juice from dandelion stems stained your hands. It was like "grasshopper spit." Holding a grasshopper loosely in your cupped hands you advised it that it must "spit tobacco" before you would let it go. Bloodroot stained, too, with its orange-brown blood.

She sat with her friends at the edge of the playground among the tall grasses and made daisy chains or pulled their white petals away one at a time, chanting, "He loves me. He loves me not," hoping that the last petal was a "loves me" one for that was the one that counted. You may not know then who "he" was, but some day you would know. And the daisy foretold his faithfulness.

Here, where the grass was tall and tough, you held a blade in a certain way between your thumbs and blew on it to produce a kind of squeaky whistle that made you shiver. You must hold it just right, though, or it wouldn't work. Buttercups grew here, and when you held the bright petals under your chin there would be a soft yellow refection on your skin. This meant that you were fond of butter. One day in August when the sky was bright blue and cicadas rasped their monotonous song; a day when birds hid silent from the heat among the leaves, she walked into a cornfield. There had been cornflowers along the roadside, but only a few, and she knew there would be more stark blue among the tall corn like ragged rounds of sky. The corn was "as high as an elephant's eye" and anyone walking along the road could not see her. When she emerged with her blue bouquet she was horrified to see a praying mantis on her skirt, looking up at her with its hard, round eyes. They were evil eyes. They could cast an evil spell if she stared into them. She shuddered convulsively, violently brushing it off as she ran.

The names of the flowers, the names she knew, were lovely to speak or to pronounce silently in her mind: butter-and-egg, windflower, Indian paintbrush, pussyfoot and pussy-willow. There was a wild morning glory and a wild colombine that had another funny name, jack-in-trousers. A jack-in-the-pulpit preached in the rich, damp woods, and Queen Anne's lace stood high among roadside flowers like elegant crocheted collars.

There were so many, always enough to gather in bouquets and arrange with a bit of fern in jelly glasses. They soon wilted, there on the kitchen window sill, but there were always more. Best of all were the violets, long-stemmed and purple-blue, gathered in a misty hollow beneath the tress. When they wanted to know where she found these special, perfect blossoms, she would never tell. It was one of her secret places.

Literary
Reflections

THE WHITE DRESS

"I could not bear to live aloud," wrote Emily Dickinson. In fact, it would seem as though the poet could hardly bear to be visible. She watched life from her "smallest room" with the door slightly ajar so she could see and hear without being seen or heard. Then one day she put on a white dress and wore it for the rest of her life.

But Emily was not a true recluse. She was a shy, introspective soul and, like many of her temperament, she wanted desperately to be noticed and loved, or at least admired. Rather than helping her to become less visible, the white dress affirmed her existence and shone her into the curious view of the townspeople like a white dove on a black bough.

The way I understand Emily Dickinson, she early created a self-image and gradually fitted herself into its outline rather than the other way round. The other way would have been the more normal one: we are first our natural selves and the image we project shapes itself around us.

Ah, but she was such an enigma. Who knows? When she first wore white to the occasional party, as did many young girls of her time, she must have seen how it emphasized her dark, soulful eyes and beautiful shining hair. These were the striking features of an otherwise plain countenance. And as she drew back into herself over the years, cringing from a real or imagined hurt, agonizing in schoolgirl crushes (long after she was a schoolgirl), the white dress was a kind of declaration of self. The unloved, unnoticed child will misbehave in order to draw some concerned attention to itself. Emily must have been aware that people in a town where everyone knew everyone else would notice and wonder. And wonder acknowledges mystery.

Critics have put labels on white as a symbol of purity, virginity, innocence. One interpreter of Emily's choice suggests she chose it deliberately as a symbol of enigma and withdrawal. It annoys me when critics make theories out of speculations and force into existing molds the interpretation that most pleases them. Emily found that her white dress brought her the attention that, in spite of her denials, she craved. She wanted to be a visible loner. I think it was as simple as that.

And then — the size of the "small life —
The sages — call it small —
Swelled — like horizons — in my vest —
And I sneered — softly — "small"!

Emily's withdrawal from society was partly neurotic and partly esthetic. Quite obviously she suffered from agoraphobia; a disorder that sometimes arises from an inability to cope with one's life experiences. In Emily's case, that might have been because she was an exceptional child in the first place, drawing curious glances and amused smiles from her associates. At Mount Holyoke Female Seminary her unsociability, her diffidence and her wit — individual and sharp — soon began to arouse comment. In one poem she acknowledges this social gap:

'Tis the Majority
In this, as All, prevail —
Assent — and you are sane —
Demur — you're straightway dangerous —
And handled with a Chain

Emily left the school after a year to return to her home on Main Street in Amherst.

There were a few visits after that to various cities: once to Washington (for her father was a lawyer and a congressman) and to Philadelphia. Over the next several years she ventured less and less frequently, and finally refused to leave her home at all.

The soul selects her own society —
Then — shuts the door —
To her divine Majority —
Present no more

A young woman, Mabel Loomis Todd, wrote of Emily: "The character of Amherst. . . . A lady whom people call the 'Myth!' She has not been outside of her own home in fifteen years! She dresses wholly in white, and her mind is said to be perfectly wonderful!"

We know from her poetry that her mind *was* wonderful, unique. The intensity of her work is extraordinary when we know that she experienced no passionate love affair or tragedy. Several biographers have offered to us likely objects of her devotion; one has even suggested a lesbian relationship. But the evidence put forward for any of these is so flimsy that it is no longer acceptable. Her talent for self-dramatization provided her with vicarious emotional experiences that we know never happened.

So Emily put on a white dress and withdrew. In a letter to an editor, Thomas Wentworth Higginson, she wrote, "I do not cross my father's ground to any house in town." Her correspondence with Higginson was initiated by herself, not because she sought publication but that she might show her poetry to some knowledgeable mind who might give her understanding and sympathy. Her letters were like the outpourings of a romantic schoolgirl, and though the editor responded it was not in kind. He did see that the strange young woman was a true poet whose writings were full of startling poetic metaphors and original expressions. Emily refused to allow him to publish those poems she had sent to him for his criticism. Several years after her death there were discovered, tucked away in her bureau drawers, booklets she had fashioned to contain 1,776 of her strange, sensitive yet intense poems.

Like many others of her admirers, I am more intrigued with the persona of Emily than with her writings. The imagery is delightful but the meters are choppy and eccentric. It's like tasting a rich creamy dessert and finding it lumpy and irritating. I love to imagine Emily, the eternal child, moving silently about the garden of her home, an almost ethereal figure against the bright, flowering shrubbery and the formal evergreen hedge. Occasionally she ventured outside the garden to the meadow beyond, where daisies and buttercups grew and a little stream pursued its meandering course. She observed nature with a poet's eye. Her tiny pale hands picked bouquets while birds and creatures of field and stream inspired her with lovely imagery: "rhythmic slim" (of a snake), "the Bumble of buzz," "the goblin bee," "Speech — a prank of parliament / Tears the surf of nerves."

I reject all the learned, psychological theories that attempt to explain Emily. To me she was a gifted, shy, intuitive personality who sought escape from the harsh world in a return to childhood. That's something I can understand.

A TORCH FOR THE DROWNING

Margaret Fuller was one of the idealistic free-thinkers who gathered at the Peabody home on West Street in Boston in the 1830s. She was an awkward young woman. She had heavy features and her eyes squinted up when she read. Oliver Wendell Holmes once commented on the "sinuous movements she made with her long, flexible neck." I suspect that many derogatory remarks made by Margaret's male contemporaries stemmed from a suspicion expressed by a later distinguished scholar: "Margaret Fuller could actually think better than a great many men."

Nathaniel Hawthorne said that she had "a strong and coarse nature." Poe called her "a detestable old maid." And Horace Greeley made the infuriating suggestion, as many men have made before and after him, that what Miss Fuller needed was a good husband and two or three bouncing babies.

Even so, Margaret was one of the attractions at the Peabody home, in the front room overlooking the street, where Mrs. Peabody and her daughter Elizabeth sold foreign books — German and French, Latin grammars, mythology, and poetry. Everyone knew that the book shop was much more than the name implied. It was more of a club where ideas of "the new age" (doesn't every century have one?) were presented and discussed. Margaret had what were called her "conversations" here. It seems to me, as I read about this remarkable woman, that she knew more about almost everything than anybody else in her day, and formed her own opinions. Schoolgirls coming into the shop to buy various classroom items that were kept in stock took as long as possible with their purchases in order to catch a glimpse of Margaret and hear snatches of her wit and wisdom. Although they sometimes made fun of her appearance and mannerisms, they recognized that hers was an exceptionally brilliant mind. There was something about her — some indefinable quality — that held one in awe and admiration. It must have been the same sort of reaction experienced by that coterie that surrounded Samuel Johnson as he held forth in a London coffee house, although Margaret would be pleasant to look upon if compared to that strange, dear, clever, often misunderstood genius.

Margaret was the first of nine children born to Dr. Timothy Fuller and his wife, Margaret Crane Fuller. Because the latter was never well even when she didn't happen to be pregnant, Dr. Fuller took over the major parenting chores of his first born. He had hoped for a boy but bore his disappointment graciously and proceeded to bring her up as though she were one. This meant that she would receive the best education he could provide. His daughter was to be "heir of all he knew" and then some. The child was scarcely more than a baby when she began to study Latin grammar. She was reading Latin authors at the age of six.

Education was all. Social graces, feminine accomplishments, the art of the hostess, were a waste of mental energy. The child was under continual pressure to excel, to fulfill the ambitions of her father. He was not without heart and did express affection towards her, but that was secondary to the attainment of perfection in everything he sought to teach her. It is no wonder that, as a young woman, she never seemed to fit in, was gauche and unable to relax in company.

Although she was a failure at friendly, casual conversations, she could hold her own with the learned minds of her day and come out ahead in many an intellectual argument. Men were afraid of her. She had been kept in virtual isolation for most of her growing-up years, then suddenly appeared among the literati of her day like Minerva springing full-grown from the brain of Jupiter. They had never seen anything like her.

It must have been Dr. Fuller's intensive training and his determination to produce a daughter of superb learning that prompted Margaret to begin asking questions about women's place in the world. Why, she demanded, were women deemed unable to absorb the same education as men? It seemed that the skills they did learn were only of use to be put on display in the drawing room, where they received patronizing attention. Learning was better, she contended, than a clean house; conversation, witty and profound, more to be practiced than graceful handling of the teacups. She was a feminist and a suffragette before the labels were familiar. It is strange that her name isn't better known today in a world where the rights of women are so important an issue.

When I made my first visit to New England many years ago, I fell in love with the country and its literary history. Without that, and subsequent visits, I'd never have heard of Margaret Fuller though she had been a prominent figure in mid-19th century Boston, and her influence continued to be felt in the growing American women's movement. She was able to express her views more widely when she went to New York in December 1844 to become literary critic of *The Herald Tribune*.

Margaret must have learned early, through a kind of osmosis, that her father attached little importance to the tender emotions; that they must be sacrificed on the altar of intellectual growth. How she strove to please him! Suppressing her girlish desires for friendship, love, personal beauty, she decided that she was going to be "bright and ugly." She may not have been as ugly as she supposed, for one acquaintance described her in a journal as having dancing eyes, excellent teeth and a thick mane of blonde hair.

The effort Margaret expended in disciplining her feelings resulted in a constant inner conflict. She suffered often from headaches, digestive troubles and nightmares. Inevitably, her pent-up emotions sometimes broke through in an explosive outburst. She erupted with wild enthusiasm for new ideas, and romanticized naively over several role-model figures, male and female. Of these passionate attachments she wrote "These loves are purely intellectual and spiritual."

In 1846, when Margaret was thirty-six years old, she was invited by friends, Marcus and Rebecca Spring, to travel with them to Europe. Thus she realized a life-long dream that had been thwarted several years before. Her inquisitive, critical mind observed, and she took voluminous notes of all she saw, for Horace Greeley had agreed that she should act as foreign correspondent for *The Tribune*. Armed with letters of introduction, she met many prominent literary people, Thomas Carlyle being one of the most popular. In France she made the rounds of the museums, attended the theatre, and found her way to the sympathetic household of George Sand, a fascinating experience. She wrote: "George Sand needs no defense but only to be understood, for she has bravely acted out her nature, and always with good intentions."

Margaret's final sojourn was in Italy in 1847. Here the uprising against the Austrian yoke was gathering momentum and Margaret found herself a deeply sympathetic supporter. When General Nichlas Oudinot, under orders from Louis Napoleon, laid seige to Civita Vecchia just outside of Rome, Margaret offered her services to an emergency hospital where she devotedly attended the wounded. Here the true tender qualities of her nature were allowed full play. Glowing reports have come to us of her gentle care of the men, and of her popularity with them.

But before this event took place, Margaret had taken a most unexpected step, one that surprised many people at home and shocked others. The date is uncertain, but somewhere between December 1847 and the following April, Margaret married the Marchese Giovanni Angelo Ossoli. Apparently the date was kept secret because Margaret was pregnant when the ceremony took place. This was no blessing from heaven to her. It seemed to mean the end of all her hopes for reforming the world, especially for helping to bring about the liberation of women from centuries of bondage. Who knows whether, with her strong will and determination to be mistress of her fate, she would have overcome every obstacle and been successful in the way she longed to be and as her father aspired for her to be, continually growing in character and knowledge.

We have no answer to this question. In the year 1850 the boat on which Margaret, her husband, and child sailed for America was shipwrecked at Fire Island and all three perished in the disaster.

I write about Margaret Fuller not only because I admire her qualities, her passion for knowledge, and her strength of character. I feel she should be better known today for her championing of the feminist cause and her efforts to point out to the world the ways in which women had been oppressed and denied the opportunity to develop their potential. In 1839 she had contacted many of the well-educated women of her community and persuaded them to meet regularly to discuss what they might do to raise the status of their sex and to break through the barriers that thwarted them. This was the beginning of her "Conversations," which continued for five years. The impact of these "conversations" was considerable, and expanded gradually throughout the whole country. Her book, *Women in the 19th Century*, gives us a history of this enterprise. It's a publication that is meaningful to us today and deserves a wider recognition.

A ROOM CALLED DUSTY ANSWER

There's something about that room, the room upstairs at Mrs. Dalloway's. Most women will recognize its peculiar quality, emanating from a fusion of nostalgia, historic shadows of old frustrations and oppressions, passionate, sometimes Gothic, tales unfolded in the formal, discreet style of the Edwardian and Victorian female author. The name, Dusty Answer, is the title of a book by Rosamond Lehmann who quotes George Meredith: "Ah, what a dusty answer gets the soul / When hot for certainties in this our life." The room was conceived and designed by Donna Vittorio who, with co-worker Janice McAlpine, operates this interesting book store.

It was one of those hot, humid days last July, and Janice came to me with a heavenly glass of water, full and sparkling with ice. I was sitting on the floor, rapturously leafing through the old books, researching for this column. But my eager concentration would have been the same whatever the purpose. Some of these authors were living when I was a little girl and I read them as soon as I was able. Skipping over the big words didn't prevent me from following the dramatic plot through to the prescribed conclusion where virtue is rewarded and wickedness punished. As for the authors, they might have been from another planet for all the thought I gave them.

Years later, however, I gave them a great deal of thought and became intrigued by the personality behind the pen. Now as I look through the old volumes, some in their original bindings, I see the work as a whole; the writer, her contemporary society, and the limitations it placed on subject, style, and free expression of her genius. To break through the barriers at all took courage and dedication.

I admit that initially it was nostalgia that held me enthralled there in the warm twilight of that upper room. I remembered the impact of some of those sentimental stories on this young reader, curled up in a Morris chair in the parlor. Novels for young people were full of saintly women with adoring daughters; of domineering men such as we find in *The Wide Wide World* by Susan Warner. My mother, most of whose reading was the Bible and Charles Dickens, loved that one. I did too. Not so long ago I tried to reread it and gave up about a third of the way through. In the same category of saintly females are the Elsie books by Martha Finlay. *Elsie Dinsmore* (her soul will surely rest in peace) is the initial volume of a series, many of which are here on the shelves of Mrs. Dalloway's, for the brooding nostalgic.

Worn copies of the famous Brontës are here, and the equally popular Jane Austen, classics that continue to appear in new editions from time to time. You will find as well other, not so easily procurable titles; for example, *Cranford*, by Elizabeth Claghorn Gaskell. The daughter of a Unitarian minister, she married a minister of the same faith in 1832 and the books she began to write were signed, simply, Mrs. Gaskell.

Others of her century on Mrs. Dalloway's shelves also believed that the use of their married names would make them more acceptable to the general public. There was Mrs. Henry Woods, author of *East Lynne*; Mrs. Hemons, nee Felicia Dorothea Brown, poet and playwright, but known best for her short poems "Casabianca"and "The Landing Of The Pilgrims." Older readers will recognize from their school days, lines from the former: "The boy stood on the burning deck / Whence all but he had fled." The work of fiction called *Cicely Brown's Trials* was authored by a "Mrs. Prosser." There was the Samantha series; *Samantha at the World's Fair, Samantha Among the Brethren, Samantha at the St. Louis Exhibition* by Marietta Holley, who preferred to be known to readers as "Josiah Allen's Wife." This series stands, among other precious out-of-print books, in a glass case, with a notice to the potential buyer to "handle with care." They are irreplaceable.

Other authors well known to all of us thought it wiser to adopt masculine pen names; e.g. the Brontë sisters were first published as Currer, Ellis and Acton Bell. Mary Ann Evans assumed the pseudonym George Eliot. French novelist Aurora Dupin presented her work to the reading as George Sand.

There is a comment in the book *Elizabeth and Her German Garden* (by "Elizabeth") that illustrates the discriminatory attitude early female authors had to contend with. Minora, an author, is copying remarks made by her host. "I rather think that is a good touch," she replied. "It will make people think a man wrote the book. You know, I am going to take a man's name." Obviously Minora felt that a man's name would carry more weight than her own.

Some other out-of-print volumes that you'd do a good deal of searching for to find elsewhere, if you could find them at all, are *A Popular History of the United States* by Mary Hewitt, published in 1860 by Harper Brothers. Also several historic novels by Charlotte M. Yonge. On the flyleaf of one old book, *Heartsease or The Brother's Wife*, I spotted this note of identification; Intermediate Class / 1st Division, Scripture Recitation Prize / Florence Lockerby, Montreal, June 1892.

I find it interesting to read the occasional inscription, to know to whom the book was presented and why. Nellie McClung's *Sowing Seeds in Danny* was presented to George Manson, RR 3, Seeleys Bay, Ontario in the '30s. *Dred, A Tale of the Great Dismal Swamp* by Harriet Beecher Stowe was a gift to "June Pearson, Sault Ste. Marie from Daddy, May 1915." Margaret Stewart wrote her name on the flyleaf of *Lady Audley's Secret* on Dec. 25, 1910. The author, a Miss M.E. Braddon, also wrote a self-deprecatory story which she titled "Just As I Am or A Living Lie."

It's impossible to include in one column all of the treasures I found in the Dusty Answer Room at Mrs. Dalloway's. There are biography and travel and "little literary magazines." In a publication called *Verse and Reverse* by the members of the Toronto Women's Press Club, I was surprised to see a contribution by Charlotte Whitton, that tough but tender-hearted politician, former mayor of Ottawa. Her sincere concern about the ills and disparities of our world are expressed in two poems; Old Houses and A Ward Prayer. You'll find inexpensive second-hand copies of works by Vera Brittain, Sylvia Plath, and Katherine Anne Porter. Prominent on the upstairs shelves are many Canadians, including Nellie McClung, Lucy Maud Montgomery, Margaret Atwood, Alice Monroe, Margaret Laurence.

My favorites of all the books offered for sale in that unique upper room are those I read and loved as a child. Even though my bookshelves at home are packed full, with books sticking out at angles and piled every which way, I had to buy several: *The Little Lame Prince* by Dinah Maria Mulock, *The Secret Garden* by Frances Hodgson Burnett. *Kilmany of the Orchard* is an old favorite of mine. I didn't become acquainted with the other famous titles by Lucy Maud Montgomery until I came to Canada. One book that always set me to laughing, and still does, is *The Peterkin Papers* by Lucretia P. Hale. Perhaps one of the reasons I bought it was that the Peterkins, in their ridiculous dilemmas, always turned to "the lady from Philadelphia." She invariably came through with a simple, common-sense solution. Being a native Philadelphian myself I was pleased to know that the "cool, practical voice from outside" that brings "a breath of fresh air and good sense" had that Philadelphia twang.

So many treasures packed into that one small room upstairs at Mrs. Dalloway's! If you don't see that certain beloved book you've been looking for so long, wait awhile. New *old* books are constantly arriving. There's a good chance that you'll find it there eventually.

THE RABBIT-HOLE

When the Mad Hatter, in his top hat with the price tag of 10/6 still on it, asks Alice, "Why is a raven like a writing desk?" she replies that she believes she can guess the answer. The March Hare then interrupts with some curt remarks on saying precisely what one means, not simply believing or guessing, and we never do learn the answer. At the time of the 1896 edition of *Alice in Wonderland*, readers thought that Lewis Carroll might be trying to generate interest and speculation by withholding the answer, but the author entertained no such motive. The riddle, he said, had no solution at all. It was part of a spontaneous narrative begun one summer afternoon when Alice and her sisters, with Carroll, took refuge from the glare of the sun on the Isis River in a meadow under a hayrick. The little girls teased Mr. Dodgson to "tell us a story," and thus began the famous tale of the Wonderland and Looking-Glass worlds.

So much has been read into Alice by analysts who poke, like spelunkers, into every psychological nook and cranny they can find, looking for hidden motives. Writers are people, and they can't help expressing their personalities in their writings any more than a thief can keep the telling whorls and arches from his fingerprints on stolen goods. But Freudians come up with a reversed Oedipus complex and "oral aggression"; some literary critics label it an allegory; others see political connotations (e.g. orange marmalade as a reference to William of Orange and Protestantism). Certainly *Alice* is full of symbols, but it is not a symbolic tale in itself. To quote the author, "I had sent my heroine straight down a rabbit-hole to begin with, without the least idea what was to happen afterwards. And so, to please a child I loved (I don't remember any other motive), I printed in manuscript — the book I have just had published in facsimile."

The symbolism and the puns are irresistible and must have been doubly entertaining to readers of that era. One of my favorite episodes is the "mad tea party." Here the Mad Hatter is concerned with his watch, whose works have become jammed with butter and crumbs. "You shouldn't have put it in with the bread knife," he grumbles to the March

Hare. His readers would have been reminded, by Tenniel's illustrations, of one Theophilus Carter, an Oxford furniture dealer who invented an "alarm clock bed" that woke the occupant by throwing him out on to the floor. Carter, at Carroll's suggestion, was Tenniel's model for the Hatter.

Alice would have understood the grinning Cheshire Cat whom she met after leaving the Duchess's kitchen. A phrase often used in her time was "a grin like a Cheshire cat," and cheese was sometimes molded in the design of a smiling cat. As the cat fades slowly out of sight with its grin remaining for several minutes after the rest of it has vanished, Alice says to herself, "I've often seen a cat without a grin, but a grin without a cat! It's the most curious thing I ever saw in all my life." In this remark I doubt that Carroll was consciously giving us a description of pure mathematics, as someone has suggested. It's a catchy phrase that might have popped into any quick-witted, imaginative mind. He didn't talk above his little listeners, and the delightful conundrums, puns and sayings that reflect the mathematician's thought patterns appear spontaneously on a child's eye level. So there are symbols and allusions, but let's not interpret this fanciful tale as the Freudian outgrowth of a "tulgy" subconscious.

Alice is contemporary, as ageless as her own dream of Wonderland. The image of her turn-about world conceived by Lewis Carroll in 1832 is ever reflected in the looking-glass of Time. I was very young when I first encountered the White Rabbit and stumbled behind him into the rabbit-hole. And though I enjoyed it then, it wasn't until my adult years that I fully appreciated this unique writer's creative genius. Now there isn't a day goes by that some phrase, some incident doesn't bring to mind a wisp of Carroll's wise nonsense. It must be so for readers all over the world. This is why I was deeply gratified to learn that a memorial to Carroll, or Charles Lutwidge Dodgson, has been given a place in the Poets' Corner of Westminster Abbey among the literary great. Even so, as Alice observes as she races in position beside the Red Queen, no matter how fast we run we never pass the trees and meadows of the Wonderland world. Its curious dream-like terrain never changes nor fades away.

A QUIET, LITERARY RETREAT

The Dormouse at Lewis Carroll's Mad Tea Party observed, just before he fell asleep and was stuffed into the teapot, "You know, you say things are 'much of a muchness.'" Well, so they are. It is only when they become too much of a "muchness" that one looks about frantically for some respite, for a quiet place; perhaps a weekend's retreat in the tranquil halls of an old monastery. Traffic sounds rise to clamor, protest marches grow violent, and bombs exploding in countries far away echo in our living rooms.

Most of us have some temporary shelter where we go to catch our breath and give our frayed nerves time to knit. More often than not, it is a retreat with no walls and no access save by way of thought and memory. Some of us go to certain books that we have read over those earlier eras that they describe. We are the lucky ones, who can lose ourselves for an hour or two in the lovely lands of the past as given to us by journalists and historians long gone away.

Mid-19th century New England is my place. Did I live there in some former existence? For I feel so at home on the village streets of Hawthorne's Salem, travelling to Cambridge now and then for a lecture at Harvard or pausing on the Boston Turnpike to share transcendental thought with Emerson. Thoreau wouldn't have invited me to his cabin in the woods, but I know the place well and I can hear the whippoorwills "chanting their vespers upon the ridgepole of the house," or the owls, in which Thoreau "rejoiced," hooting in the twilight woods when I read about them in his *Walden*.

It is their serenity of spirit that beguiles me; those transcendentalists whose energy of intellect didn't cause them to become "hyper" — as one might say today — but rather give them a composure that is seldom encountered anymore. I know one or two such souls. But they are rare. It is the contrast between this steel-hard, computer-technological age and the gentle, metaphysical flavor of the middle years of the last century that attracts, so that sometimes I wish I could wander so far into the interior that I forget my way back.

In a way that was far different from the "cool" disguise so admired and adopted by certain young people today, those transcendentalists were real "cool cats." Base passions waned in the rarefied atmosphere where their minds liked to soar. Certainly they were human and loved and had families about whom they cared (though maybe forgot them on occasion while in pursuit of some high-flying metaphysical bird). If that isn't the way humans should be, that, nevertheless, is the way they were. At the same time that they acknowledged their bodies, they tried to deny their carnal natures; they didn't like to admit that their limbs were flesh and blood.

If wild passion existed in the New England heart, it was successfully suppressed, perhaps to surface in some less intense eccentricity. Hawthorne's profound love for Sophia Peabody could scarcely be described as "hot and sexy." Margaret Fuller did, we read, get a bit over-emotional, in spite of her preoccupation with matters of the mind. But she sailed away to languorous Italy and found there a Latin lover who pleased her in a way the cool New Englanders could not.

Most of all I like to retreat to the Salem of Hawthorne's time. It's quiet there or hushed, rather, for "hush" has a different quality than "quietness." There is a secret tension, as though one waited for an immortal word to be spoken. Twilight in Hawthorne's Salem frightens me a little because, although nothing sinister actually happens, it always seems *about* to. There is the sweet beckoning of melancholy which we love to obey, however well we know the pain in its tenderness.

Everyone took long walks in that New England era, like those English poets who were forever taking to the mountain trails and the paths that skirted the meres of the Lake Country. Everyone talked metaphysics in a climate that was harsh and astringent, exciting the literary mind.

That is where I like to go when the world is too much of a "much-ness." I join my friends on the New England highways and byways while we contemplate truths that are timeless and universal. The rarefied air revives me and sweeps from my brain today's metallic dust and smog. Perhaps on one of these walks I'll go along home with Nathaniel Hawthorne to that somber house on Herbert Street in Salem, and take a room beside his, under the eaves.

THE TENANTS OF DOVE COTTAGE

It was in the spring of the year 1972 that I went to England to make the acquaintance of my English aunts and cousins. My Auntie Ethel Hayne and three of her four daughters were my hostesses at their home in Luton on the Kingsdown Road. They are a kind, gentle family with a gracious Victorian way about them and everything was done to make my visit pleasant and interesting.

When I planned my visit I wrote to cousin Florrie advising her of the places I wanted to see. The Lake District headed the list, most especially Dove Cottage where William Wordsworth lived with his sister for nearly a decade. Wordsworth's poetry has always appealed to me but it was Dorothy I was most interested in. My copies of her letters and journals are well worn with reading. Each page is as alive as though it were written yesterday, with her delight in nature, her charming accounts of domestic matters, her walks over Rydal Mount, with the mist rising from the hills. Then the coming home to poke the fire and make the tea. She wrote in her diary that she had gathered moss "to make the chimney gay against my darling's return." She adored William. She devoted her life to him.

When I first saw Dove Cottage I was surprised how small it was. I wondered how on earth Dorothy could have accommodated all those friends and relations who came to visit, some of whom stayed for weeks or months at a time. Samuel Taylor Coleridge, arriving for his first visit, stayed nearly two months. Later he settled in with the Wordsworths, sleeping on a couch in the drawing room, bringing along a hundred or so books for which shelves had to be found. There were occasions when he brought his son Hartley along. He called the cottage "home" for twenty years, though he was often away on excursions through England or on the continent.

Mary Hutchinson, a childhood friend of Dorothy's, often stayed for days, helping with cooking, laundry and sewing. She became a permanent fixture when she married William in October 1902. Three of their children were born there and spent their early lives there at the same time that Coleridge was sleeping in the drawing room with his books. There was John Wordsworth, a sea-going brother, who dropped in between voyages. He proved to be of invaluable help, for he built cupboards, shelves and even chairs. William, whose head was always in the higher altitudes, wasn't worth a hoot with a hammer! John was a knowledgeable gardener too. He planted trees and shrubs as well as giving time to the vegetable garden.

Dove Cottage, though small, had once been an inn; The Dove and Olive Bough. There were three downstairs rooms, the largest, which Dorothy made into a drawing, or general, living room, was sixteen-by-twelve feet, a dark oak room with diamond-paned windows and a stone floor. Of the three upstairs rooms Dorothy arranged one to be a living room for William, and furnished another for his bedroom. This would have been adequate accommodation for the two of them. But there must have been much juggling about and bumping of elbows when friends and relatives descended upon them, often unannounced; and later when William and Mary began to produce offspring.

The ever patient and loving Dorothy waited on all, washed and ironed, mended old clothes and "bound carpets", turned out cupboards. She records that she spent all one morning "making a mattress — I cut my thumb."

With indoor work done for the day to her satisfaction, she would put a goose on to cook and repair to the garden. There she "struck the peas" and weeded the turnips while William lay under the trees. "Old Mollie" Fisher, an old rustic who lived nearby, often came in for two hours a day to help. Though "very ignorant, very foolish, very difficult to teach," she was honest, and devoted to the Wordsworths.

In spite of all this domestic activity Dorothy made herself available to William whenever he wanted her to walk with him. Her accounts of these wanderings in her journals are enchanting poems in embryo, which the poet William delighted to hatch. No wonder he urged her to keep on with her writing. It doesn't seem ethical to me but Dorothy was enormously pleased when "dear William" adopted her thoughts and phrases as his own.

The Wordsworth property at Grasmere reached to the margin of the lake, though not the lake of "the daffodils". That was Ullswater. The siblings roamed, alone or with friends, for miles around the country, up and over the hills and beside the lakes that flowed between Grasmere,

Rydal. On one bright autumn evening Dorothy "walked up the hilltops" and observed that "the moon shone like herrings in the water," "the half-dead of the near-sheep bell in the hollow of the sloping combe (was) exquisitely soothing." Another summer afternoon as she ambled on the edge of a meadow while "William lay listening to the waterfalls and the birds", (seems like William was always lying about somewhere), she saw "the shape of the mists, slowly moving along, exquisitely beautiful; passing over the sheep they almost seemed to have more life than those sweet creatures." She wrote of "the unseen birds singing in the mist." She was deeply sensitive and receptive to nature. Her images are fresh and vibrant as though newly minted.

    I don't want to be unfair to William. His mind was pre-occupied with precious things: spiritual beauty and mystical experiences, the charming innocence of a child's mind, the holy silence of the world at sunset. Not the least of his precious pre-occupations was William Wordsworth himself. As I read his contemplative poetry I find myself wishing that I didn't know as much about his personality as I do. Even the adoring Dorothy realized that people weren't readily attracted to William. John Keats, while admiring his "intuitive awareness of life" found him egotistic, vain and bigoted. It's funny how two such different people can exist side by side in the same head. I'm thankful for William Wordsworth's poetry. And I remember that had he not become a major poet, I'd never have made the acquaintance of his delightful sister Dorothy.

JOURNALS OF TRIVIA

It didn't snow in the night. I was so sure it would as I stood in the doorway waiting for my little dog to come in from his last visit to the garden. There was that pregnant hush in the air, that vibrant silence that prevails when the season first tilts toward winter. I thought about last year and wondered when it was that we had our first snow. There would be a note in my 1988 diary and probably some reference to my ecstatic reaction at the time. I found it on the October 22 page. "It was a thin, gentle rain at midnight. Now, at six a.m., there are soft round flakes; our first snow." Later in the day: "Heavy slush as I slogged along to the mall; a stinging wind."

One day I was consulting a diary of several years past. A friend of mine wanted to know the date of some experience we had shared. She was surprised to learn that I had kept diaries for so many years. "I sometimes wish *I* had," she said. "But I wouldn't know what to write about. Nothing very exciting ever happens to me."

Immediately I remembered an observation that someone had made about Jane Austen's writings. "Jane Austen's stories are full of people to whom the first snow was an event." Sometimes the first snow *is* an event, I told my friend. She agreed. But it had never occurred to her to write it down. Her personal reactions didn't seem worthwhile recording.

She referred to some of the great diarists of the past whose journals have taken on the status of literature. "Most of them didn't write for posterity," I pointed out. One doesn't keep a diary with the sense of future critics looking over one's shoulder. It's for you to read over and to remember, with the same rapture only a little faded by time, that May morning when you had some early errand to do, and the fresh, sparkling glory of the hour made you catch your breath; the new sunlight on incredibly green grass, the wheel, shining with dew, of the black and yellow garden spider. Don't tell me that's not an important event. It is good to remember beauty. Surely everyone wants to remember, especially when one runs unexpectedly into an ugly day. In the years ahead you'll enjoy it many times over.

Samuel Pepys wrote only for himself. In fact he wrote in code, making sure, he believed, that this account of his private life would never be revealed to a prying public. It is true that he was witness to many important events, and historians are eternally grateful to him for his recording of them, and his shrewd observations and descriptions. For example, he was aboard the ship on which Charles II returned to England in 1660. He was a friend of Sir Isaac Newton, and also of "that miracle of a youth, Christopher Wren." We are immensely fortunate that he should have unintentionally left us these records.

The delightful accounts of his domestic life he especially wouldn't have wanted publicized. We are told that some pages of his diary, though decoded, have never been published because of their absolute frankness. My point is that he recorded innumerable trivialities simply for his own satisfaction. "I dined at home in the garret where my wife dressed the remains of a turkey, and in the doing of it she burned her hand." On one Lord's Day in September 1665: "Up and put on my colored silk suit very fine, and my new periwigg." If you have a new colored silk suit that you enjoy wearing, write it down. In the years ahead you'll enjoy it again, in memory.

Beatrix Potter began a diary when she was fifteen years old and continued it until her thirtieth year. She was the child of parents who strove to bring her up properly according to strict Victorian standards. Most of her early life was spent alone, save for a governess, in the nursery of the third floor of her home at Bolton Gardens, London. Her brother, slightly older than she, was sent away early to school. There were few outings for her and little social contact.

For many summers the family removed to a country house in Scotland where the Potters seemed to do their best to make life as dull as it was in the city. So what was there to write about? Well, there were bird's nests, and mice, and trees to climb and study. And all the animals on nearby farms. The smallest happening in the world of nature was an event to her. She wrote it down, with the comment that nobody would ever read her words. Yet, like Pepys, she employed a code that she had composed herself. It wasn't until many years later, in 1966, that the key was discovered and her journals published, to the delight of those of us who know that it's the commonplace incidents of life that matter most.

The joy of Dorothy Wordsworth's journals, her accounts of the weather, of walks with William over the Rydale hills, or alone because

William "lay abed" with a headache; her pleasure in caring for him, preparing a "Basin of broth" or a seed cake; all this trivia reminds me that there is much in my everyday life to mention in my diary. All of little interest to anyone else, but I'll read it over next month, next year, and savor again the quiet miscellany of the past.

I was fifty when I began to write regularly and seriously in my diary. Before that my efforts had been sporadic. In maturity, looking over those earlier attempts, I decided to discard them. They made me squirm. I understand how Alexander Scala felt on rereading the journals of his adolescent years. "What puerility! What fecklessness! What lousy writing! Each time I turn a page of the thing I discover a new reason for wanting to lie down on the floor and howl like a dog." Yet he continued to read. I, too, found myself horribly fascinated by my account of my own adolescence, from which I was further removed than Alex. Unlike him, I was able to bring myself to throw those diaries away. I don't need them. Memory has a way of suddenly confronting one with the most embarrassing incidents, sharp in wretched detail. And again I wince at some stupid error or idiotic behavior in front of respected, maybe idolized, elders, who are probably dead and gone by now.

However, we do learn to forgive ourselves as we grow older. Our sense of humor saves us a lot of pain. I enjoy reading over my second collection of diaries. I see how I've coped with situations that overwhelmed me in an earlier day. There are times when, not feeling well, I've almost persuaded myself that I'm "coming down with" a serious illness, that I may not be long for this world. My diary tells me that I've felt this way before and whatever it was went away without a trace. I am reassured, and I relax.

The New Year draws closer, and new calendars are on the store counters. It's a good time to decide to keep a diary. Anything that grabs your attention and holds you musing for a moment, whether beautiful, curious, or strangely poignant, go to your diary and quickly record it. If you leave it till later it's hard to recapture the intensity of that first impact. Never mind if you can't think of the right words to describe it. A few key words will bring it back, to some happy degree, in later years. And there's no blue pencil waiting to correct your copy.

Sometime you're going to read and remember; perhaps on a day when a glimpse of past pleasure, or at tears that time has inevitably dried, are all you need to help you through some fresh adversity.

CASTRATING PETER RABBIT

It isn't far from the village of Near Sawrey to Hill Top Farm where Beatrix Potter lived. One isn't sure that the past tense applies here, for Potter's presence is everywhere. There is the illusion that the householder has just stepped out for a moment to feed her friends in the farmyard.

Had I come upon the spot unadvised on a casual walk, I'd have recognized it immediately: the flagstone path leading to the cottage garden, wild roses in the hedgerows, then a random profusion of foxgloves, snapdragons and tiger lilies, lavender and Sweet William, late daffodils still holding on, and bluebells at their loveliest. Hadn't I seen it all before in the watercolor illustrations of her books? Beatrix Potter's gardens, as well as her landscapes and interiors, and especially her animal characters, are all drawn from life. She was a faithful, enormously talented but also trained artist, writing and painting directly from the nature that she loved.

Jemima Puddle-Duck was one of the ducks that lived at Hill Top farm. She is pictured there telling the other farmyard residents, "I wish to hatch my own eggs. I will hatch them all by myself." A cousin of Beatrix Potter tells how she and the artist walked about, looking for a suitable place for Jemima's nest. An illustration for this tale shows Jemima, at the artist's suggestion, considering a tree stump among a stand of tall foxgloves.

Potter's fans (and there are millions of them, for there are many translations) can recognize, as they step into Hill Top cottage, the rooms, the staircase of Tom Kitten's house. I saw where Tabitha Twitchet stood on the landing in front of the grandfather's clock. I saw the spot by the entrance hall where she received her guests.

For the story of Ginger and Pickles, Potter painted the actual village shop at Near Sawrey. The shop is a private home now and there have been changes. But in the little back room where Ginger the yellow tomcat and Pickles the terrier totalled their accounts, the old meat hooks still hang from the ceiling. Another scene from the Hill Top area is in *The Pie and the Patty Pan*: the garden at Buckle Yeat, a property close to Hill

Top, where Duchess the Pomeranian is shown reading an invitation to tea from Ribby the pussycat.

The landscapes of Potter's illustrations are easily recognized by those who have visited the original sites. When I toured the Lake Country some years ago, I saw perhaps the loveliest scenery of all, the county of Cumberland, where my favorite, Mrs. Tiggy-Winkle, the prickly washerwoman, collected soiled clothing from her furry clients. A hill called Cat Bells and the hillside path in Kelbarrow, Grasmere, where the inspiration for the little house in the hill where Mrs. Tiggy-Winkle washed and ironed.

The authenticity and the meticulous effort taken by Beatrix Potter in her sketches and paintings are never more evident than in the book *The Tailor of Gloucester*, published in 1903. The designs for the embroidery of the Mayor of Gloucester's coat were taken from tapestries at the Victoria and Albert Museum. The coat is described as made of "cherry-colored corded silk embroidered with pansies and roses, and a cream-colored satin waist-coat trimmed with gauze and green worsted chenille." Some of the original paintings for this tale hang in the Tate Gallery in London.

No less true to their models are Beatrix Potter's drawings of animals. The prickly washerwoman was a faithful sketch of the author's pet hedgehog. Hunca Munca and Tom Thumb, the two bad mice, were her favorites among her many pets, for "Beatrix Potter was very interested in mice." Her two Belgian rabbits were the originals of Peter Rabbit and Benjamin Bunny. In July 1881 Potter obtained an art student's certificate from the Science and Art Department of the Committee of Council and Education, certifying her mastery of Freehand Drawing, Practical Geometry, Linear Perspective, and Model Drawing.

All the above is by way of explaining why I was appalled to read, when I was visiting the United States not long ago, an item in *The Charlotte Observer* for Friday, September 1987. It announced, with indignation, that Ladybird Books of London has brought out a modernized, simplified version of *Peter Rabbit* illustrated with photographs of "stuffed animals with plastic eyes, stitched noses, and black-thread frowns." With their sights focused on a large potential market, they offer us the rationalization that this is what today's child sees on TV, and what he/she, prefers.

Omitted is the reference to Peter's father, who Mrs. McGregor baked in a pie. Spokesperson Pat Roth accounts for the omission by telling us "At a very young age, it's a bit, you know, traumatic." When I compare this reference to some of the cartoon violence depicted so vividly on our television screens, I can't believe he said that! And didn't he know that, though Peter Rabbit was introduced to America in hideous comic-strip-type editions, his popularity grew by leaps and bounds when the authorized English edition with Beatrix Potter's illustrations arrived on this continent?

"The important thing about Peter Rabbit [like all Potter's animal characters] was that he was alive and true to the nature of a rabbit," says Potter's biographer, Margaret Lane, which fact the children recognized immediately. How could those cute, vacuous stuffed toys be preferred to the scrupulous, authentic pictures of the actual animal dressed in clothes appropriate to its nature? Ladybird Books grossly underestimates the child's appreciation of the real thing as compared to the commercially prompted phony. My mind makes the comparison with the stage presentation of Peter Pan which I saw recently at Niagara-on-the-Lake, and the Walt Disney production. Disney's nature documentaries are truly wonderful, but his animated cartoon productions of classics like *Pinocchio*, *Peter Pan* and *Snow White and the Seven Dwarfs* make me feel like crying in angry frustration.

Surely the many lovers of Beatrix Potter will rise up to make their protest before the foul project goes any further. But it is disheartening to learn that *Squirrel Nutkin* is already off the presses, and *Tom Kitten* and *Jemima Puddle-Duck* lie under the editorial blue pencil. The art and genius of Beatrix Potter can never be smothered by the coy and cunning treatment of greedy publishers. But it's a crime to today's children to offer them this doctored, inane trash in place of the exquisite original.

LOOKING SIDEWAYS

The ominous pall of witchcraft still hung over the old city of Salem, Massachusetts, when Nathaniel Hawthorne lived there on Herbert Street. For 11 years, in a little room under the eaves, he dreamed and wrote and seemed like a kind of ghost himself, emerging each day at twilight to walk about the lonelier lanes of the town. He wasn't a gloomy man; rather he wore a soft melancholy that made him particularly sensitive to the darker aspects of the past and of human nature. From the corner of his eye, with a kind of oblique glance that he liked to employ, he saw the shadows take on familiar contours and the dimly recognized features of long-ago townspeople. He wrote in his journals of a child "flitting among the rose bushes, in and out of the arbor, like a tiny witch."

It is hard to say whether Salem was largely responsible for the forming of Hawthorne's curiously imaginative mind, or whether he enhanced for himself the more sinister aspects of that old town, haunted by the moaning protests of condemned witches as they took their last steps up Gallows Hill. He listened to the tales of Yankee sailors, read the *Annals of Salem* and often pondered over fading portraits in the museum of Cotton Mather's day.

Many times I've followed in Hawthorne's footsteps to the Hardy and Turner Streets corner and into the House of the Seven Gables, where his umbrella in the rack by the door has suddenly pierced me like a curare arrow, transporting my mind to the strange days of more than a century before. I could hear the tinkle of the bell, see the heavy door opening and this man of the brooding shadows and cob-webbed vision entering to pass the time of day with his cousin, the current owner of the gabled mansion.

Hawthorne was well acquainted with the House of Seven Gables and indeed well informed on the history of the strangely alluring city. It had a morbid significance for him, since one of his ancestors, William Hawthorne, a judge in the seventeenth century witchcraft trials, had condemned to death as a witch one Rebecca Nurse. Nathaniel felt responsible for the sins of his fathers; he confessed for them and prayed for their souls. This preoccupation with the past is revealed in his stories, full of curses, guilt, expiation. Yet his protagonists never seem to experience the relief that should come with confession and atonement. I doubt if the author himself was every really relieved of his burden of guilt.

Today many of Salem's citizens would like to forget the Witch Trials, or they contend that the stories have no more substance than superstitious legends. Others, for the sake of the tourist trade and for love of tradition, whether pleasant or sinister, emphasize and perpetuate the colorful past. Most appropriately, one of my visits there fell on Halloween, so that I felt more than usually sensitive to its peculiar history. I sat in the Common by the Nathaniel Hawthorne Hotel, feeding the pigeons and musing on those who had walked there long before. Presently I summoned a cab from the Witch City taxi company opposite and went to visit the Court House, where I was able to examine some of the documents relating to the trials.

Not everyone will find the haggish flavor so strong, as though a great cauldron of unearthly stew still simmered in the park of Gallows Hill. But its disturbing aroma still, for me, lingers unmistakably. Perhaps that is because I have always felt particularly drawn to Nathaniel Hawthorne, especially to the period he spent in this city, when his world was all shadows, observed sideways by a bemused eye; when he first knew that he was a writer and recognized what his theme would be. In those years when he lived withdrawn in his attic chamber, writing at a pine table — when days would go by without his seeing or being seen by his fellow tenants, his mother, his sisters Elizabeth and Louise — he read, studied the history and lore of the area. He had so many questions to ask of his Maker, such deep compassion for those tortured souls who had sinned in some very human, understandable way and were forever after haunted by these sins. He wanted people to understand rather than to condemn; perhaps forgiveness would prove to be their salvation. In years to come his readers would see in his fanciful tales this aching desire for acceptance for these unhappy human beings who were *fellow* human beings after all.

When he emerged from his years of seclusion it was with the knowledge that one of man's greatest sins is to keep himself apart from society, to withhold sympathy and love from his fellows. If he refuses to identify himself with this "great warm human heart" of created man, he prepares the furrow for the seed of his own misery.

*Reflections
on Nature*

TO STAND AGOG

I never could have thought of it
To have a little bug all lit
And made to go on wings.

— Elizabeth Madox Roberts,
"Firefly"

I remember when I first noticed fireflies, their tiny flickering lights punctuating the summer evening. They were fairyland creatures then, awesome but real; not bright thoughts in the imagination of an ignorant child. Since then I've read about fireflies. I've learned that their light is produced by the substances luciferan and luciferase combined with oxygen. It is a cold light they create, something that man has never been able to duplicate. And a light that resists extinction: grind up a handful of fireflies, and the pulp continues to glow.

We study our textbooks, and we learn the scientific facts behind phenomena that enchanted us as children. But all our acquired knowledge shouldn't leave us less agog. Science doesn't disenchant. The breaking-down process of analytic research can't take away the magic of the incredible facts of nature. What if the man in the moon is an illusion: is the moon less marvellous then? We learn what things are made of; the reason for a bubble; why the sky is blue; how a cricket chirps. But the amazing intricacy and ingeniousness of nature, the repeated delightful surprise of it all, and how it could even *be* in the first place, must keep us wide-eyed with awe. The crux of the mystery, as the German philosopher Heidegger put it, is "Why is there anything at all rather than nothing?"

Some lucky people never fail to look where they're going, and they don't look casually. The hummingbird beating its wings 80 times a second, hovering at the threshold of a trumpet flower, causes them to be late for work. A cat on the prowl, with all the exquisite stealth of a jungle tiger, interrupts their daily routine and puts awry the whole day's schedule. They know that if they could only understand what a flower is, "root and all, and all in all," they should "know what God and man is. "But they don't know. And so they stand, like Cortez, "silent upon a peak in Darien."

Dr. Lewis Thomas was asked to name seven wonders of the modern world to replace the ancient traditional ones. How can one select seven out of millions? However, he does give us a list of seven wonders that he finds particularly surprising and marvellous. One, not the first named, is a species of beetle called the oncideres, whose first thought on reaching maturity is to find a mimosa tree in which to lay her eggs. No other tree will do. She deposits them in a slit which she makes in the bark of a branch. But mother beetle knows that her children cannot live and grow in live wood. So she cuts another slit around the branch right though to the center, which chore takes her eight hours. Before long the branch breaks off and falls to the ground, and there the beetle children eat and grow and mate and find another mimosa tree. Lewis poses the question "Does this smart beetle know what she is doing?" But this is only one of the processes in nature that boggle the mind.

The first and supreme wonder, says Lewis, is the world itself; especially our piece of it, the planet Earth, the "strangest of all places" in the universe. "It can keep us awake and jubilant with questions for millennia ahead, if we can learn not to meddle and not to destroy."

Some days are too full of business to allow time for being agog. And a good thing too. We are forced to ignore that crafty spider spinning a web from a thread in its abdomen. Although we're aware that a song sparrow is warbling ecstatically on a telephone wire, we must zipper our ears if we're to get anywhere at all and fulfill the mundane duties of the day.

My Auntie Lily used to say about some surprising happening, "That was enough to make a body get up and sit down again." And so it was, and is — this life of ours and every little part of it from the puff ball that springs up overnight at our feet to the twinkling of the farthest star. What else can we do when confronted by the miracle and magic of it all but stand agog?

RAIN LORE

We stood at the window looking darkly out at the rain as children have for centuries, because it had spoiled our plans for the day: for skipping, for ring dancing, for laughing in the sun. We chanted, "Rain, Rain, go away. / Come again another day." We wondered why it should have come at all, for hadn't we been very careful not to squash any spiders nor to cut or pull any ferns or grasses? Everyone knew these acts provoked rain. Finally, when the rain had moved on with only a skim milk mist to mark its passing, we put on our black shoe rubbers and stiff macintoshes and hurried out to slosh about in the puddles.

"Puddle-wonderful" e.e. cummings called that post-rain world. One looked deep into them to see the tree-tops. I wished that I could explore that other upside-down place as did Alice when she stepped into the contrary realm of the looking-glass. Where cars had passed over roadway puddles iridescent stains shimmered like smears of blue or green watercolors. Worms wriggled across the sidewalk or lay flattened in the street as though pinned on wax for dissection. Translucent drops mirroring sky-tones of blue and light hung on the garden spider's web.

Folklore advises us of acts and conditions that bring on rain but has little to say for stopping it once it has begun. A black snail crossing one's path is a sure sign of rain, and should you kill a toad the clouds will burst violently above you. However, rain must happen occasionally in any case. You may predict it when you see the white linings of poplar and silver maple leaves, or when the bite of the horse fly is sharper, or when your great toe sends you the message in painful throbs of code. St. Swithin sometimes reminds us, on his day in July, that he still resents the moving of his grave from a humble graveyard to a more honorable place. If it rains on his day many look gloomily ahead to 40 days of wet weather. But early morning showers in the summertime should be greeted happily. An old Pennsylvania Dutch proverb tells us that morning showers are as short as old women's dancing. And we all know the popular prophecy "Rain before seven, sunshine by eleven."

There are times when we long for rain, however, when the parched earth assumes the aspect of a pale chocolate pudding that has been standing too long. Farmers in thirsty fields watch hopefully as a purple cloud moves on to more fortunate furrows. In primitive cultures there was always (and still is in some African and Asiatic lands) the rain-maker. J.G. Fraser's *The Golden Bough* gives us several pages of rain-inducing magic and ritual, and the rain-dance is included in many of them. Wizards of the North-American Natchez danced while blowing a spray from their water pipes towards the heavens. In Angoniland beer is poured into a pot in the ground as a gift to the Rain Spirit. Any beer remaining from the brewing (and there is always sure to be plenty) is finished off by all members of the tribe, even the children, who then dance around the buried pot. In parts of Java a pair of cats, male and female, are carried in a procession while suitable words are sung, then thrown into a pool, which act in some way appeases the appropriate gods who have been withholding vital showers. In many Catholic countries suffering from drought, holy images were tossed (or thrown angrily, if the supplicants were becoming impatient) into water to compel the Deity to help in their extremity. In modern times many people have found, myself included among them, that rain is sure to fall within hours of washing one's car.

Henry Thoreau liked rain. But then Henry rejoiced in any natural phenomenon that men couldn't interfere with. It enhanced his solitude. "The gentle rain which waters my beans and keeps me in the house today, is not drear and melancholy but good for me." And should the rain become a deluge, "There was never yet such a storm but it was Aeolian music to a healthy and innocent ear." When looking out, one becomes profoundly aware of home as the dearest shelter imaginable; the familiar walls and furniture, the kettle on the boil, the blue bouquet in the Wedgewood vase, the depth of the silence measured by the ticking of the clock: all these blessings grow indescribably precious. To quote Thoreau further: "I sat behind my door in my little house . . . and thoroughly enjoyed its protection." In his eyes the rain was never a mixed blessing but always a full and desirable one.

POETS IN WINTER

In this our winter there come back to me cameos of past winters, moments or eternities, that might have been announced with a fanfare of trumpets or seared into my skull with a branding iron. Yet there were no startling visible events to recall them so vividly. They evoked, perhaps, the same emotions that arose in John Keats as he "stood tiptoe upon a little hill" and looked upon a scene so still that "not the faintest motion could be seen," not a leaf fell. Yet it was a moment of deep import, so compelling that he wrote a memorable poem about it. The same profound impression was received by William Wordsworth, walking along the grassy shore at Ullswater when he came upon those famous daffodils. It was a brief visual experience that was to flash over and over in time upon the "inward eye" of his memory.

I can't explain why one or two scenes of long-ago winters should rise above the long, flat landscape of time to return with such clarity and poignancy. Nor why I should have been more aware at one precise moment rather than another. I was walking home one winter evening from a late school program, briskly, to keep warm in the freezing temperature; reviewing in my mind the answers I'd written on a difficult test paper. Suddenly the utter silence hit me as though a drum had sounded beside me, and I stopped abruptly as at a command. I've never *heard* such silence! There was a sense of a great heart beating, a throb felt rather than heard. Snow from the previous day's fall lay quiet on the fields on either side, frozen to a glistening crispness. Inches above the macabre silhouettes of bare, black trees the stars shone with a brightness possible only in the clear air of winter. I stood utterly still, caught in a mood of ecstatic wonder. It was as though I knew, in that interval of time, the answers to all my questions, the fulfillment of all my inexpressible longings. I was aware of knowing, though there were no words to define what I knew. Perhaps this was *sensucht* in the sense that C.S. Lewis used the word in his autobiography, *Surprised by Joy*.

This quality of silence and timelessness is a phenomenon that belongs more to winter than to any other season. When the snowstorm is over, soft dunes and purple shadows lie across the earth, and branches scratch the sky with the stark eloquence of a Japanese print. A poetic form superbly suited to the description of a winter landscape is the Japanese haiku; a form that was, in its inception, simply the poetry of the seasons. Basho, perhaps the greatest master of the haiku, captured, as though in amber, this mood of profound stillness and tranquility in fifteen syllables: "The first snow, / Just enough to bend / The daffodils." His disciple Joso, also writing in the seventeenth century, expresses the same Zen concept of the moment: "Fields and mountains, / All taken by the snow; / Nothing remains."

Many Canadian poets, not surprisingly, write of winter, in lines that often have a quiet, mystical flavor. Perhaps our greatest national poet is Archibald Lampman, whose last poem, "Winter Uplands," was written a week before his death on February 8, 1899; a strangely prophetic sonnet of great beauty:

> *The frost that stings like fire upon my cheek,*
> *The loneliness of this forsaken ground,*
> *The long white drift upon whose powdered peak*
> *I sit in the great silence as one bound;*
> *The rippled sheet of snow where the wind blew*
> *Across the open fields for miles ahead;*
> *The far-off city towered and roofed in blue*
> *A tender line upon the western red;*
> *The stars that singly, then in flocks appear,*
> *Like jets of silver from the violet dome,*
> *So wonderful, so many and so near,*
> *And then the golden moon to light me home;*
> *The crunching snowshoes and the stinging air,*
> *And silence, frost and beauty everywhere.*

WINTER ALBUM

Although they had seen it for six or seven winters, it was as though they were seeing it for the first time: a world white and silent and strange, though not alien. At first, walking into it, they seemed reluctant to raise their voices, as one might hesitate to speak out in a cathedral's sacred silence. Then the astringent cold stabbed their blood to action, and they began to move about, lifting their knees high to walk through purple-shadowed drifts.

Shortly after sunrise they had been fortified by big bowls of oatmeal porridge that had been sitting on the back of the stove all night, so that a crust had formed and had to be stirred in. They ate it hurriedly but with relish, because it was covered with rich milk and maple sugar or syrup, and their stomachs knew it was good. It kept them warm as they spelled out their names in footwells where the snow lay deep, wind-side of the snow fence. They lay on the smooth ermine of the front lawn to brush out patterns of angels' wings with their arms. Later they would admire their artistry from the wide front window as they sipped cocoa from thick china mugs and munched on cookies lumpy with raisins.

It was a time of knitted toques and mufflers — "clouds" as some called them — and mittens. No nylon snow-suits insulated with poly-ester, but ribbed stockings laboriously drawn up over long-legged under-wear and over these, for outdoors, mackinaw socks that tied above the knee. Over feet already heavy with woolen wear were slipped moc-casins or shoe pacs made by Grandmother from deer skins she had tanned herself. Moccasins were cosy enough but, being heelless, not too secure, and the little ones fell down a lot. It didn't matter. Snow was for falling and giggling.

Bright winter afternoons, when they breathed cloudy puffs into the air like miniature steam engines and one had to look squint-eyed at the glinting snow, they took up their skates and tugged along with older brothers and sisters to the frozen lake. Their bobskates were like little sleighs, two runners in front, two behind, and were strapped on to boots or moccasins. The older ones wore "store-boughten" skates that clamped on and could be adjusted to hard boots with a key. They glided and slid and tumbled and bumped like frosted tumbleweed and yipped like happy puppies. Into the farmhouse kitchen then, rosy and weary, where Mother helped strip off frozen togs. These hung about the stove for hours, steaming and smelling in the warm air.

Some winter nights are silent chiaroscuros, white figures against night skies, windless and spectral. On such nights Father might gather up fishing gear, rods and poles, pork rind for bait, and chop holes in the ice where there just might be hungry perch or pickerel, trusting creatures who believe it's God up there dangling their dinners. Sometimes as an unexpected treat the little ones were privileged to go along. There might be several fishing holes, and over each stood a forked stick, line dropped down into the water and pole weighted firmly on the ice. When several bobs jiggled at once there was great excitement to land the big one before it got away.

There were bobsledding afternoons when a sledding snow had fallen throughout the night. Then it was up the hill puffing, down the hill squealing, a big boy piloting while the youngsters hugged each other's waists rigid with delicious fear. More often they pulled home-crafted sleds made from pine or cedar boards with runners covered with strap iron. Then one Christmas they found under the tree a store-bought sled with metal runners shining like icicles in the sun, slats glazed bright yellow with red trim and the glorious name The Flyer painted across the end.

That's the way it was for someone I know who was once a little boy and remembers when snow drifts were higher and winds were colder and you took a "pig" to bed to warm the icy sheets. Perhaps he would give you a lot to have those old times back again. But if it means relinquishing his electric blanket, forget it!

THE DARLING BUDS OF MAY

Last year and the year before May Day dawned dark and cold. Hardly a time to go a-maying or leaping about in diaphanous scarves as did the young folk in the old Roman Floralalia. I'm writing this in mid-April, keeping my fingers crossed, and hoping that the forecasters in the *Farmer's Almanac* have misread their weather signs. May 1st and 2nd, they tell us, will be cloudy and cold. However, things look better through the remainder of the month: weather warmer than usual with not much rain.

What delight the old Greeks and Romans took in the spring. They practised what Omar Khayyam recommended: "In the fire of spring / Your winter garments of repentance fling." Nature gave them all they needed to celebrate — the warmth of the sun, the intoxicating, balmy breezes, sprays of wild hyacinth and myrtle to wave as they bowed and skipped and sprang into the air in the fresh, green meadows. Now, instead of garlands of flowers we grab a cooler, pack it with sandwiches and beer, get in the car or line up in the railway station, and head for a couple of miles of beach on the outskirts of town. There we spread out a blanket, set up our beach chairs, eat and drink and, "let it all out." We have a "great" time.

But sometimes in the middle of a sandwich, we pause. We gaze out across the water to the horizon, and there comes to us a kind of sad hesitation of the spirit, a moment of yearning for some quiet country we cannot name. Somewhere out there, over the water, we see a glimpse of peace, a climate infinitely desirable. And then it is gone. And someone says, "Hey! Can you open this bottle of ketchup for me?"

The coming of May still makes us happy. We still go looking for wildflowers; the hepatica under its furry leaves, the pink-veined spring beauty. The ancient Pagans did the same and called it "a-maying." They gathered hawthorne blossoms and windflowers. They chose a "Queen of the May," sat her in a little arbor and paid homage to her with singing and dancing. They were drunk more on spring than on wine. Spencer wrote of the "yougthes folke," — they haste the postes to dite / And all the Kirks pillours eare day light, / With hawthorn buds and swete eglantine — "the postes" being the maypoles. These were festooned with garlands and ribbons and the celebrants danced around them until they could dance no longer. There are still maypole dances. I remember taking part in one on a Field Day at school. We held the ends of ribbons that were attached to the top of the pole, and weaved in and out in a folk dance routine. The result was supposed to be a beautiful pattern of woven colors covering the pole from top to bottom. However, the dance I took part in turned out to be utter havoc. Some of us inned when we should have outed or vice versa, and we ended up with a riot of pink, blue, and yellow snarls and lumps. One would have thought a Roman Bacchanalia had taken place.

The ancient revelers were deprived of their maypoles when the Puritans complained that the dance was a pagan rite and an insult to the Christian church. A sixteenth century Puritan named Philip Stubbes wrote that they brought home a tall pole, drawn by "forty yoke of oxen, every ox having a sweet nosegay of flowers tied on the tip of its horns, and these oxen drew home this maypole (this stinking idol rather), which is covered all over with flowers and herbs . . . And they fall to banquet and feast, to leap and dance about it, as the heathen people do."

So a stop was put to their revelry. Now, in the areas where it is occasionally observed, there's neither Christian nor pagan connotation. As far as I was concerned at my school, it was a weird and wild exercise. Dressed in my middy blouse and floppy gym bloomers, I stumbled in and out among the dancers, totally ignorant of what I was supposed to be doing.

If we only had time to enjoy May more, and space to enjoy it in! When I had a back yard I knew something of the joy those old Pagans felt; the Greeks especially loved the flowers, for their land was all stony mountains and rock-studded fields. They noticed, and rejoiced when the bleak bluffs came alive with the bright burgeoning of spring.

There are other events in May to invite our observation besides the flowering of the earth. Whitsunday, or Pentecost, often occurs in May. It used to be the favorite time for the Morris Dance until it was suppressed, again by the Puritans. That, too, has been revived in some countries but no longer does it pay tribute to pagan deities. It's simply an expression of the exaltation we all feel, human and beast alike, at this happy season.

Then there's Mother's Day. A lady named Anna Jarvis of Philadelphia proposed it in 1907. It seems that no one in Congress dared to vote against it. Our card merchants and florists are forever grateful.

May is the time to eat dandelion greens, if you like dandelion greens. And apiarists, look to your bees. For "A swarm of bees in May / Is worth a load of hay." One historical event that shouldn't be overlooked is that on May 22 in the fourteenth century, in Bavaria, women were given the right to duel men to settle disputes. Apparently there were some champions of women's rights even then, who would demand their rights at sword point.

Now, having written all this, I hope that May will be kind to us this year; that "rough winds do (not) shake" its "darling buds." I remember snow in May. But the *Farmer's Almanac* doesn't forecast snow for this year. They know whereof they speak. Being students of meteorology, they don't put their faith in woolly caterpillars.

FIRST THE SEED

At seventy-three one ought to be able to do as one likes, within reason, that is, and always regarding the feelings of others. When I picked up the digging fork and headed toward that clayey bit at the end of the garden, Jeff jumped to his feet. "No! No! You shouldn't do that," he protested. "I'll do it when I get home from work."

I looked at him and decided there was no use arguing just as he was leaving the house. "OK," I agreed, with my sweet-old-lady smile. I gave him five minutes before I continued with my purpose, which was to turn up the aforementioned clayey bit at the end of the garden!

It wasn't easy. In fact, it wasn't possible. Ninety-three pounds of pressure just wasn't enough. I moved close to the garage and by balancing myself with one hand, I mounted the fork with both feet. It didn't do at all. I kept falling off.

I hate giving up but I realized the job would take more ballast than I could supply. Anyway, I consoled myself with the thought that Jeff would be pleased with me for leaving it to him. He likes making himself useful. Besides, there were other, less strenuous chores to be done.

The old cliché about the healing therapy of working in the soil is true. So often I've proved it. Breaking up the clods of earth with my hands, digging little holes with the trowel for the comfortable bedding of some new impatiens plants is better than "a couple of Aspirin and call me in the morning." You forget, for a time, that nagging worry that had been lying in your chest like a lump of undigested cheese ever since you woke up, because you remember the way the delicate red and white petals shone under the hedgerow last summer. And now it is spring again and you're still here and putting in a garden as you have for so many springs.

I'm not much of a gardener. My garden prospers by luck and by the grace of God. I've never been accused of having a green thumb. But sometimes one loves a thing even though one may not be good at it, and the response turns out to be more than is deserved. And then, I tell myself as I nip off the dead pansies so fresh blooms will come, the unmerited rewards are threefold; physical, esthetic and spiritual. There's a fine distinction between the second and third blessings that would take several columns to define.

Having given up on the stubborn ground at the back I go to a flower bed along the front porch. This plot I've fed and nurtured for several years, and the soil is rich and loamy. My purpose here is to plant two clematis vines. I do love clematis but somehow have never tried growing it before. When I was very young I read a story about a little girl called Clematis who wandered away from her home to explore the world; who lived in the woods and the meadows, making friends with the wild creatures who had their homes there. How I envied her. It all seemed so possible. I even wished that my name was Clematis instead of plain old Mabel.

Following the instructions that come with the plants, I dig two holes eighteen inches deep, throw in some bone meal, a good splash of water, and set the clematis in. It takes me a long while. My arms become tired and achy and I perspire a lot. But I feel fine in my heart, peaceful and excited at the same time. For I can see the mature vines twining up the trellis, spilling over onto the porch their pale mauve petals. I know they will be as lovely as the pictures on the label.

I break up the earth with my fingers in the way that I blend flour and shortening when preparing pie crust. There's the same sort of pleasure in both tasks; both are creative in the same satisfying way. One must admit, however, that there is more lasting joy in a stand of lemon lilies than in a wedge of lemon pie.

When we lived in the village of Sandhurst on the Bath Road, I used to watch my elderly neighbor, Mrs. Robinson (her name was Mabel too; I wonder if she minded) on her knees in the garden, patiently weeding between the rows of flowers and vegetables, for hours. I asked her how she could keep it up for so long; didn't she get very tired? And she'd just smile and say she liked to do it; it was restful. She meant peaceful, perhaps; the kind of peace I'm finding now, absorbed in the moment as I press nasturtium seeds, like hard, wrinkled peas, into the earth. I like the astringent smell of nasturtiums, and the lily-pad look of their leaves.

Though it is warm it occurs to me that some coffee would go down well at the moment. I pour it into my favorite mug and sit on the back steps to drink it, looking about with eyes that see the potential; the full-blown flower beyond the green sprout. I note how the forsythia has survived her first nervous year and is aspiring to be a golden princess in another spring. The Rose of Sharon breathes healthfully beside some languishing narcissus; another reminder of my childhood when I could see its flowers like dark, winy hollyhocks, against the kitchen window. We called it the "rose tree." I paraphrase a haiku (there is one for every aspect of nature):

I am one who
sips her coffee
gazing at the Rose of Sharon.

The day moves on and I remind myself that the lovely garden in my head won't come about if I spend my time drinking coffee and dreaming. So it's back on my knees on the good earth where I find that there is, in the making of a thing, as much fulfilling pleasure as in the contemplation of the finished work.

SMALL WORLDS

I like small: microcosms that suggest infinity, but don't boggle the mind with gargantuan forms and distances. Not long ago I stood on the south rim of the Grand Canyon looking down into the sculptured depths of that vast chasm, its temples and forts and terraces. Tiers of buttes and craggy sills stretched for miles, ranging in color from the predominant smokey brick through parchment buff and chocolate brown to a wood-violet blue in the shadow. Although my eyes took in the scene my mind could not assimilate it. It was like trying to eat all at once a marble layer cake as big as a breadbox.

Lilliputian landscapes suit me best. Everything is there, all of the spiritual and physical components of life existent in miniature. Small is comprehensible, and because it is it teaches us more of the eternal truths than Big ever could. Alfred, Lord Tennyson, addressing a flower that he had plucked from a crevice in a wall, said, "If I could understand / What you are, root and all, and all in all, / I should know what God and man is."

I prefer Few to Many, for Many overwhelms, but One can be understood and held. The solitary tree on a hill has leaves with design and color to be identified and admired, but its identity is lost when it grows amid a great blur of forest. I love nooks and crannies; the way a small clump of brittle reeds lays its silhouette on the sand where one can mark a water beetle's track through the dappled shadow. Thoreau wrote of cuddling down "under a gray stone [to] hearken to the siren song of the cricket." Lying in the grass, observing the scene from a rabbit's eye level, I've watched a polka-dotted ladybug climb to the very peak of a swaying grass blade, or tried to outstare a savage-eyed preying mantis. In winter one can explore filigreed frost patterns on the glass canvas of a north window; and I've discovered that the needles of the Colorado spruce have gems of frost on their tips like six-pointed stars.

C.S. Lewis loved hiking and took many walking excursions, one of which was a fifty mile tour over the hills and valleys of Exmoor. Although the mountainous scenery impressed him with its grandeur, he disliked heights and would leave his companions to explore smaller areas at lower altitudes. In so doing he began to give more notice to smaller things: a single flower, the way a stream curved where it changed course. "I gazed down into a little ditch beneath a grey hedge where there was a pleasant mixture of ivies and low plants and mosses." He wrote of having "a stronger sense of the mysteries at our feet where homeliness and magic embrace one another."

To contemplate the more intimate aspects of nature is to see life with a childlike perception. The secluded nook at the edge of the garden has an arched doorway of spirea, and beyond it is a quiet, secret place where you can stand hidden by slim Lombardy poplars. You will note the way the sun slides through ever-tremulous leaves, dancing and shimmering on the dark grass. The four-leaf clover won't escape your gaze, and you'll know where the song sparrow mothers her young in a low thicket.

Small is warm and charming, ingenious and simple. It illustrates profound truths with Lilliputian imagery. As William Blake wrote:

To see a world in a grain of sand
And a heaven in a wild flower,
Hold infinity in the palm of your hand
And eternity in an hour

A SUMMER PLACE

The lane to our old cottage had the quality of a cathedral close, embowered with leafy branches. Sunlight, filtering through leaves, suffered a kind of sea change and glowed like a pale green haze, from which we emerged on to a terraced bank. Here we looked down 100 feet or more to the lake. On our first visit I felt like Thoreau when, at the age of five, he had his first glimpse of Walden. "That woodland vision," he wrote in his journal, "for a long time made the drapery of my dreams."

The nature of the light around and in the cottage was what first impressed me, and that is what "flashes upon the inward eye" when I remember that summer retreat. Trees stood close about the house, so that we seldom had bright sunshine. I bought thin orange scrim for curtains, and the light sifting through made matte gold patterns on the floor. At times, late summer afternoons, when birds were quiet in the heat and the lake lay still, one seemed to be suspended in a kind of golden twilight.

There's a soft maple on the grassy terrace and a small stand of birches at the edge of a pine wood. Nearer the lake are tag alders; willows bend over to nod at their reflections, and the quaking aspens continually quiver, though no breeze may be blowing. One evening as we came from fishing and drew in close to the dock in our small boat we saw dozens of bullfrogs squatting on the lower timbers, silent, staring with bulbous eyes like so many gargoyles. What were they doing there, all together, mute and paralyzed as though under a spell? Were they all princes waiting to be kissed?

A green grass snake lived under the back step, whose name, my husband told me was Sniveley. (Jack knows these things.) Sniveley seemed a happy snake, coming and going regularly on his reptilian errands, whatever they were. But one day we saw him slithering with an agitated wriggle at an unaccustomed time, and we realized that something under the house had disturbed him. It was a woodchuck family. We saw the rear end of a little one heading for home, then its face, as it turned to look at us and give an angry, nervous whistle. Another day we found it backed up into a corner as though afraid to dash for the safety of its burrow. I talked gently and tried to make friends, but you can't make friends with a woodchuck, although Edwin Way Teale tells of carrying on a kind of whistling conversation with one. This baby was a tough one, baring its teeth and snuffling like a small dragon.

We thought it was a snow goose we saw one morning as a large white bird glided down and settled half-way across the lake. We approached in the boat and were within a few feet of it when it took off and headed north, but we did see the black wing tips and knew we had guessed right. Everywhere we walked chipmunks zigzagged across our path. Squirrels were a constant comic relief, running in and out of the stone curbing, teasing the dachshund, who would race toward them only to hear them a moment later chittering impudently from behind.

The biggest house spider in the world lived in my bedroom at the lake cottage. Although I've admired the black-and-yellow garden variety out of doors, marvelled at the geometrically perfect web and wondered at the confounding ingeniousness of the Creator, it was hard to praise God when I opened my eyes in the morning and spied a creature big as a tarantula (it's true!) glaring at me with unmistakable malevolence from the window sash. Another house-mate, not so repulsive, was the little deer mouse, who didn't worry me at all except when she made a nest in the dresser drawer, all cosy and warm among my red flannelette pyjamas.

The hot summer sound of the locust was one of the voices of our cottage country. In the evening called the whip-poor-will, and I have answered him until he has come to the terrace where I sat. But the true and distinctive voice of the northern lakes is the cry of the loon. Weird, lonely, sounding over the water on a still evening or in the spooky haze of dawn, it makes one uneasy, apprehensive of we know not what impending doom. Yet I wish I was hearing that sound again, and the flirtatious invitation of the whip-poor-will. I long to see Sniveley; the bullfrog gargoyles under the dock; even those sinister eyes of the devil-spider; to move and dream again in the golden twilight of that summer place.

SEPTEMBER SONG

Edna St. Vincent Millay, contemplating summer's swan song before the trumpet blast of a New England October, wrote, in that mood of dove-grey melancholy that was always a part of her personality:

Gone, gone again is Summer the lovely.
She that knew not where to hide,
Is gone again like a jewelled fish from the hand,
Is lost on every side.

Millay, known as Vincent from childhood (she was named after St. Vincent, patron saint of the sick), conceived the lines on the Vassar campus where she was to publish her first slim volume, *The Buck in the Snow*. An ecstatic greeter of spring who could write, "Bobolink, you and I, an airy fool and an earthy / Chuckling under the rain," Millay was nevertheless more at home spiritually in the mists and airs of September, when the dust of country roads lay on the white upland aster and dimmed the bright blue of a wayside cornflower. Vincent's schoolmates knew her as fun-loving, elfin at times, giving a light, fanciful touch to their intercourse with an imagination that went from the sublime to the fey.

At the same time they were aware of brooding depths, a preoccupation with some mystical vision that inspired her poetry. She wrote of autumn, not looking ahead to a splendid finale of scarlet and gold and copper, but sadly backwards to a gentle season of warm indolence and love in the sun. It was always love expended, flowers faded, or glories lost in the dark, cool auguries of winter. There *was* one poem she wrote in praise of autumn, one of my favorites, that begins, "O World, I cannot hold thee close enough." but here, too, the emotion experienced is more pain than joy, a cry that earth's beauty is sometimes more than one can bear: "Lord, I do fear / Thou'st made the world too beautiful this year."

Such poetry, sentiment if you will, so popular in the early decades of this century, is out of style now. Emotions don't change, but literary fashions do. We must be hard and severe now, touch the wound with a styptic pencil, deny the sublime and define those sentiments that stir our hearts with words that are clinically accurate and realistic. I once had the great good fortune to discuss poetry with Dr. E.J. Pratt, and when I mentioned Edna St. Vincent Millay in phrases that must have been close to adulatory, he referred to her work as "emotional stomach noises." Perhaps I was hurt at the moment, but later, thinking it over, I understood his opinion and concurred with my head if not with my heart. E.J. Pratt is a great poet with an international reputation whom I admire unreservedly for his objectivity, his strong, clean, epic lines, an overall quality that I must call integrity. Millay is personal, introspective, a young girl passionately in love with life, constantly being burned by its searing beauty and prepared to resist death, as she says in Moriturus, "Shrieking to the south / And clutching at the north."

There were times, however, when Millay could see beyond her personal emotional reactions, and those times help give her credibility to posterity, whatever literary winds blow. She was deeply concerned over the rise of Nazism, concerned for the safety of "England, France, and my own country," and wrote stanzas that were published in newspapers and in pamphlet form by *Harpers*, intended to awaken people to the increasing dangers of dictatorship. She lent her talents to raising money for Chinese and Czech war relief at a time when she was suffering the agonies of a persistent neuritis and public appearances were a torture to her.

But now, when summer moves into its old age with petals fading from purple and scarlet to dingy browns, and bird song dies on September winds, I remember Edna St. Vincent Millay, her reluctant farewells, her wistful, nostalgic lines to "Summer the lovely . . . / Lost again like a shining fish from the hand / Into the shadowy tide."

THE NATURE HIKE

Once a week in the spring and summer, when the sun shone and soft breezes stirred the meadows of blue and purple clover, we schoolgirls put on our khaki gym bloomers and middy blouses and went for a nature hike. Our sneakers laced above our ankles over brown cotton knee socks, and as we set out two by two behind our guide we might have been a bevy of rollicking female students from St. Trinians. Miss Endrie headed the line like the figurehead of a galleon; some thought her a bit horsey, but I, inclined to the most unlikely of crushes, thought her magnificent. We tramped across the winding road of the campus, down the gravel track that bordered the swimming pool area, passed the dark doorway of the artesian well that we referred to as King Tut's Tomb and entered the cool, exciting woods.

We had come to this place to find the first wild flowers of the season, delicately veined spring beauties, velvet-stemmed hepaticas couched in the soft leaf debris, may-apples under their flat green umbrellas. When it was daisy time in the June meadows we found, in the open woods, wild Sweet William and Jack-in-the-Pulpit. The competition was keen to find the most unusual specimen of wild flower or to gather a greater variety than anyone else, and to this end we scrabbled among the squishy mulch of last year's fallen leaves or muddied our white sneakers in the swamp reaching for cattail spikes. Flower picking is something children will do naturally for the love and wonder of it, and they do it simply and innocently. Not so, however, with Miss Endrie's fifth graders. This was a race, ruthlessly competitive; the reward being high marks, one's name in the school paper and last, but not least for me at any rate, the teacher's approval and praise. There were ugly snarls as greedy fingers met over a rare find; restrained grumbles that later, in the junior dormitory, would break out into open warfare. We did not query, as did Emerson on coming upon the fresh Rhodora in the woods, "Whence is the flower?" Rather, it was "I saw it first. It's mine!" and "Get your cotton-pickin' fingers off that dog-daisy!"

I remember . . . I remember — in spite of the intensity of one's infant passion to excel, to escape in some way one's drab anonymity — quieter moments in those luscious woods. One day I climbed a forbidden fence, posted "No Trespassing," walked through a kind of cedar copse and came upon a little hill covered with Quaker Ladies. There they stood, a whole colony, the palest of blues with tiny yellow eyes, low to the ground and demure as their namesakes. They belong to the bluet family; perhaps their regional name derives from their appearance in Philadelphia, the Quaker City. Then there was the day someone (alas, not I) discovered a walking-stick like a bent straw on an oak leaf; so well camouflaged, the insect isn't easy to see. Of wild-life specimens we saw only the occasional rabbit, woodchucks, sometimes a skunk (which we fled, screaming). Once, to our wild excitement, we heard the baying of hounds, and as they approached we had glimpses through the trees of scarlet-coated hunters, the West Chester Country Hunt Club, riding by on the high road. Without exception we were on the side of the fox. Although they couldn't have heard, we yelled in unison, "He went *that* way," pointing in the opposite direction.

But it was specimens of leaves and flowers we had come to find, and presently we gathered up our treasures and started back to the school house. We itched from mosquito bites, stung from scratches suffered in our explorations. (Or were they battle scars?) Invariably, some would wake the next morning swollen and itchy with ivy poisoning. We sang as we trudged back up the gravel path old camp songs such as Be Kind To Your Web-Footed Friends, The Trail Of The Lonesome Pine and a school ditty, Ellis Will Shine Tonight. We were tired and hot and starved and happy.

And that's how it was in the buttercup days of the jolly, nature-loving schoolgirls of Ellis College, class of '34.

THE GENTLE CROC

The smile on the face of the crocodile doesn't persuade us that it is anything but nasty and treacherous.

How cheerfully he seems to grin,
How neatly spreads his claws,
And welcomes little fishes in
With gently smiling jaws

is the way Lewis Carroll put it. So it amazed me to learn that the female of this species, whose bite is so perfectly meshed, who could take one's leg off like a guillotine's blade, handles her eggs and hatchlings with the utmost tenderness. Should some be slow in breaking through the shell, she responds to their little hiccough-like chirps by holding the eggs in her mouth and nicking them ever so carefully to help the hatching. We see Mother Croc in a recent TV documentary in this maternal activity, after which she fussily conducts all her little ones to the water.

It isn't difficult for us to imagine the TLC a dainty, white-soxed deer mouse provides for her young. But we do get a bit of a jolt when we discover that Mother Bat, about whom most of us feel a bit squeamish, is the most attentive of parents, nestling her child in the fur of her stomach, recognizing its squeak of alarm when trying its wings among other fledglings, and snatching it to her protective body.

One can remind oneself of the realistic reason behind this moving maternal behavior in most living creatures: the reproduction of one's kind and the necessity to nurture offspring to the age of fertile puberty. In some creatures that cold, stark fact is all, and obvious. In others, sometimes most unlikely ones, there is a tenderness that beguiles us to the belief that mating and maternity are more than cold reproductive processes; that there's something else that looks very much like the emotion of love.

Is it possible to attribute tender feelings to so unattractive a creature as a crab? William W. Warren, in his book *Beautiful Swimmers*, yields to that temptation and persuades us by his sensitive writing to agree with him. The female of the Atlantic blue crab has several molting periods, the final one being the most difficult for her and coinciding with her brief time of sexual availability. For at least two days before actual mating takes place the lucky male who finds her makes a kind of protective cage over her, and when she lies exhausted and naked and most vulnerable to attack, he cradles her, shielding her from harm, sometimes for several days. Only when she is fully recovered from the molting experience does her spouse enter her and then remains with her another few days, continuing his protective role. Warren writes, "It is a most affecting scene" and refers to this cradling as a "tender quality" unique among the species.

Most of us know from TV documentaries and our reading that elephants have a great capacity for affection. This information, however, fills us at first with delighted surprise, for we tend to associate tenderness in animals with the smaller varieties. The young elephant receives loving care not only from its parents but from uncles and aunts as well. As it walks along close to the flank of its mother it frequently feels the reassuring touch of the maternal trunk or the caressing nudges of other adults. More unusual among animals is the herd's concern for an ailing member who falls along the way. They stay with it, pushing and prying to help it back on to its feet, giving up only when the situation seems hopeless.

The incidence of tenderness among nature's wild creatures is a moving sight, though I may be guilty of antropomorphism. If love in the wild is nothing more than a beguiling ruse to trick all life into reproducing its kind, then so be it. It's a lovely ruse. But I'll bet you a dollar to a dolphin it's more than that.

Canadiana

OUT OF THIS SEED

The lady in the linsey-woolsey gown and the cotton poke-bonnet, with her infant in her arms, sat down on a hill and cried. This land at Sorel, Quebec, looked desolate and wild, with only a few scattered wooden huts to indicate that any human life existed here. She was ill-prepared for pioneering in a strange country. It had been possible to bring only a few of her belongings, household necessities, even clothing, along with her. For it was the year 1783, and she, along with others loyal to the British crown, had been driven from her home in the fledgling United States, her property confiscated. It was an outrage to be compared to the expulsion of the Acadians from Grand Pré and Chignecto thirty years earlier, when the British military ordered homes to be burned and the beleaguered French-speaking residents herded on to ships to be deposited in the swamps of Louisiana. Fortunately these United Empire Loyalists, as they came to be called, had been promised good farmland grants immediately west of Fort Frontenac, and it was in that area that they arrived in the year 1784, under the leadership of Captain Michael Grass.

It was tough going at first, an experience requiring extreme fortitude and physical stamina. But that was what they had, and they persevered and flourished. Our young mother entered her tent home, supplied by the British government, swallowed her tears and proceeded to make out of a length of canvas a livable dwelling. From the government, too, came some clothes, household implements, tools; never enough, but the will to survive stimulated the imagination to greater ingenuity than they dreamed they possessed. Ignoring the old adage, they learned to make silk purses out of sows' ears and soon replaced tents with log cabins. As early as the summer of '85 an official wrote that the Loyalists had made "much greater improvement than could be expected in so short a time." And the Rev. John Stuart, writing from Cataraqui, reported, "The town increases fast, there are about fifty houses built in it, and some of them very elegant. . . . We are a poor, happy People, and industrious beyond Example."

The warmth of the first log homes didn't cause the occupants to perspire profusely in the severe winter weather, especially where the windows were oiled paper and the door a blanket. To satisfy healthy appetites they added to their rations of flour, pork and beef, root vegetables from their cleared land. Their manna may have come from heaven, but they didn't gather it up as easily as did the Israelites in the wilderness. They searched for it in the woods and plains; the black and red raspberry, the small wild strawberry. "Dandelion coffee," wrote Catherine Parr Traill, without enthusiasm, "is little inferior to good coffee." And sweet fern made a "not very unpleasant tea." Fish, of course, was plentiful, fresh and unpolluted: perch, bass, pickerel. Before the settlers harvested their own hops, their barm was made from salt, flour, and milk, with which they baked salt-rising bread. In the leaner winters they shared soup bones, boiled by one family after the other to the shiny smoothness of elephants' tusks.

Indians taught them how to tan deerskins to fashion boots, dresses, and trousers, and they grew flax to be made into coarse linen. There were a few grist mills in the area, an early one at Napanee, but many had to crush their own grain under wooden pestles or stones.

Kingston, benefiting from the industry of the loyalist transplants from south of the border, grew quickly. By 1812 it was described as "Upper Canada's largest and most important center." As early as 1785 it had a school, a post office in 1789. In 1808 there was a stage coach travelling between Kingston and Montreal; in 1819 a regular steamship service to York and Niagara. The King's Town accessibility by land and water was an enormous asset and contributed to its rapid growth.

Our pioneers, not only the Loyalists fleeing from harassment in the U.S. but from whatever reason, built us a country out of berries and nuts and logs, flax and deerskin, common sense, and communal fellowship. Underneath it all, generating the human machine and nurturing the spirit, were incredible courage, vision, and hope. Those qualities have not been lost from our genes; they remain as strong and sure as ever, available to us in times of great stress and painful confusion. Like now.

SO MOTE IT BE

Although there will be added cause for celebrating this July 1st, what with our Constitution coming home to roost, eh? or at least trying to hold itself together on the parliamentary perch, I doubt if our revels will match those that took place in the early days of Confederation. The pride and excitement that inspired George Brown's special "Confederation Day" article for the *Globe* in 1867 was to bubble up in the hearts of Canadians with the same effervescence for years to come. Will Canada Day '82 glow with that kind of patriotic fervor, inspire spectacular parades, and burst into pyrotechnic bloom in North America?

It is true that the day our Constitution came home was a grand one. And I, along with thousands of others, couldn't help but be moved by the pageantry and the pride, the patriotic good humor among the crowds, especially when the rain began to fall. It is to be hoped we will remember.

On the day of the signing of the BNA Act in 1867, cannons roared congratulations, bonfires flared, church bells rang out. In the other four provinces that composed the Confederacy — Ontario, Quebec, New Brunswick and Nova Scotia — the weather was sunny, fine for parades and for gathering in squares and marketplaces to hear the reading of the official proclamation. After the cheers had died down, families went on picnics or watched boat races or found some special way to mark the special event. The annual repetitions of these celebrations prompted an 1880 issue of the *Canadian Illustrated News* to comment, "We believe it is unprecedented that within so short a space a day should come to be regarded as a National holiday in the full sense of the term."

Canadians of early Confederation days welcomed this new holiday eagerly as another occasion to escape from their daily labors, which often kept them occupied from dawn to dusk, although the gruelling workday was gradually diminishing from 12 hours to 9. Now they would have more leisure time, what with their evenings and Saturday afternoons. One of the popular ways to celebrate Dominion Day was to jam into an excursion boat and paddle-wheel away to a local beach or picnic ground.

They may have had to "swim for their lives," as noted by the *Bystander* in 1881, but it was all very jolly and exciting. Railway lines offered special excursion rates on this and other holidays.

By the 1880s people were enjoying more team sports, and organized leagues were coming into existence. But the old ball game on a town sand lot or a cropped pasture in the country, whose players were neighbors or picnicking relatives, was most popular. An editor of a Christian publication worried that the increased interest in sports was "destroying the intellectual habit of the nation. . . . There was no time left to read the heavier literature, or to follow intellectual pursuits."

Any excuse to have a picnic was seized with joy, and what occasion could be more fitting than Dominion Day? Of course there were parades. If some couldn't get to the cities or towns, well, they'd make one of their own with local fifes and drums smartly leading the way and the rag-tag-and-bobtail procession, enthusiastic, blissfully out of step, following behind. Fireworks after dark were as dazzling as could be managed. If you didn't have elaborate sky-rockets or "Pharaoh's eggs," you touched your match to a Catherine wheel or a Roman candle. The little ones ran about with "sparklers" like fairies in the Athenian forest.

However one feels about the ways and byways Canada has followed since Confederation, whatever one's political philosophy, the fact is that Canada was born. It happened. One can't but be grateful for that and see to it that our celebrations come on strong and clear. Sir John A. Macdonald and George Brown, for once in accord in their dream of a great united nation, may seem to some naively idealistic. But without ideals a dream never gets born at all. As Brown wrote in his July 1st, 1867, edition of the *Globe*, "The people. . . who shall hereafter inhabit the Dominion of Canada . . . shall, under a wise and just government, reap the fruits of well-directed, honest industry and religious principle . . . in the blessings of health, happiness, peace and prosperity. SO MOTE IT BE."

HELEN'S SON JOHN

John A. Macdonald stood on a table at his home in Glasgow, Scotland, and made his first speech at the age of four. What he lacked in eloquence he made up for in dramatic gestures — so much so that he wheeled off to the floor, banging his head on a chair. It was a speech no more lively and impressive than many another he gave during his long political career.

Helen Shaw Macdonald always believed (and didn't hesitate to say so) that her son John would "make more than an ordinary man." The second son of the Macdonalds, William, had died in infancy; and one day in May of 1922 little James, the third son, fell and died while being chastised by a servant who was minding him. Both Hugh and Helen Macdonald dreamed of great things for their remaining son, but it was Helen who saw to it that he continued in school and kept to his studies and whose personality and love had the greatest influence on his life.

John as a small boy in Glasgow was a lively child, full of fun and energy, always ready to join in the games that children played together. There was one rowdy game played with long sticks called "shinties", with which a ball was driven between two opposing sides. There were marbles, called,"bools". And "Charlie over the water", in which one dashed madly across the street, trying to avoid being "tigged". Young John played hard and slept hard and didn't like to get up in the morning. Later in life, though plagued by various ills, frequent colds, bronchitis, gallstone attacks, and other pains that he was neurotically sure were cancer, he remained energetic and cheerful, entering each day's arena with headlong enthusiasm.

John was five years old when he came to Canada in 1821; first to Kingston, then to spend a few more years of precious childhood at Hay Bay and Glenora, about forty-five kilometers west of the city. It was delightful country in which to be a child. There were trees and woods for rambling, for building Scottish castles out of the stuff of memory and imagination. Here flowed the waters of the Adolphus Reach, northward and westward to the Bay of Quinte. And high up in the middle of a shadowy wood lay the mysterious Lake on the Mountain, a lake that set a small boy's mind to pondering, for there was said to be no bottom to it.

Fish swimming in the waters of Hay Bay apparently desired nothing more than to be caught on a fish hook. But the young lad's first "catch" was a black bass flapping about wildly on the bank where an old resident, "Guy" Casey, had tossed it. Excited out of his wits, John grabbed it in his arms and ran off, deaf to Casey's outraged shouts. Sir John later turned the incident to his advantage on the speaker's platform.

Although young John Alexander loved the out-of-doors and unorganized play, he was an avid reader. Study and school were no problem to him. While living at Hay Bay he trotted willingly enough the three miles along country roads to the school at Adolphustown. John Hughes, "Old Hughes", was the *dominie*, a tyrant remembered for his harsh rebukes and birchings. Though the boy put his mind to his lessons and learned quickly, he was the instigator of much mischief. But also adept at talking himself out of the consequences: a convenient talent for a future politician.

It was when Hugh Macdonald decided to make the move to Prince Edward County to operate a grist mill there that John went to stay at Lodgings in Kingston to attend the Midland District Grammar School, a heavy expense for his parents. But they knew their son to be destined for high things; as his father had said of him from the beginning, "There goes the Star of Canada. . . . Ye'll hear something from Johnny yet."

A happy childhood is a precious thing. Imagination makes an exciting chamber in the mind, revealing so many doors to be opened, so many worlds to explore. But if there is no love, there is no happiness. John A. Macdonald had both love and a lively imagination as a child. He grew to be a man of insouicance and humor, with a deep understanding of his fellow man. All of which qualities made him by no means perfect. No one ever seriously claimed him to be an angel. But his faults were more weaknesses than misused strength, more wit than malice. If he dealt the astringent blow, he also received the same with good humor, laughing with his detractors. It would have been no surprise to his mother that he became the first prime minister of Canada. Helen Macdonald always knew he would "make more than an ordinary man."

REFLECTIONS ON CANADA DAY

Having declared that I know all the words to *O Canada*, and can sing them in my piping tenor, without hesitation, I was awarded my certificate of Canadian citizenship in 1973. I mastered the national anthem without undue difficulty, having struggled all my life with the awkward range and rhythm of *The Star-Spangled Banner*, a formidable piece of music for a voice that is not comfortable outside of middle C and its dominant fifth. Although I'm not averse to learning another language I was relieved that a working knowledge of French wasn't required. I must add, however, that through my many years in this country I have familiarized myself with the peculiar idioms and syntax of the Canadian vernacular and can ooze forth a soft rising "eh" at the end of a sentence as easily as a native.

That "ooze", however, I still spell with a "zee" in the effort to retain a modicum of American accent. When I tell my friends that I caught a "mowse in the howse" they remark that I speak English almost as well as a Canadian and have nearly lost that leisurely Philadelphia twang.

My Canadianization is further affirmed by the fact that I can distinguish Wayne from Shuster, and have a sincere admiration for the beaver. I still prefer baseball to hockey but I believe the sport most popular with Canadians to be a noble and manly one, "eh?" I've a fondness for fiddleheads and I eat a bowl of maple syrup every spring no matter how much I dislike it. My tendency to feel guilty about almost everything is no deterrent in my effort to adopt the Canadian character. Pierre Berton once defined a Canadian as one who knows how to make love in a canoe. Fortunately that wasn't mentioned in my citizenship application but were it required I'd be willing to learn.

There is much more to becoming a naturalized Canadian than such frivolous considerations, of course, and I took the step with all due seriousness. My home has been here for many years and the people have shown consistent kindness towards me. I admire the Canadian reserve and the impression of sincerity that it signifies. My roots are in the United

States and one doesn't stop loving one's homeland but I'm grateful that Canada has accepted me as a citizen, and I strive to be a good and loyal member of my adopted country.

Millends

SOMETHING SENTIMENTAL

It was a pretty calendar, sentimental and bright, with its shining butter-cups of pure cadmium yellow, and its chalk-white daisies. The artist must have painted the scene at noon, for the light lay evenly upon the flat meadow and there were no shadows. "It's pretty," Erin said, with the indulgent smile of a teenager who believes she knows a thing or two about art. "But it's calendar art. No subtlety. The color goes on right from the tube." I knew that she was right and that in my admiration I was showing my naivete and ignorance. "Nature isn't like that," Erin went on. "Take the landscapes on some of those old calendars: bright pink and gold, and purple mountains. They're for sentimental old ladies who like 'pretty' better than 'real.'"

One day when spring had almost slipped into summer and the sun had coaxed all "the darling buds of May" into full bloom, my sister and I walked to our favorite place to pick our first wild flower bouquets of the season. We came up behind the Indian Rock in Wister Woods, from which we had our first glimpse of the meadow across the boulevard. A pretty and sentimental scene, one had to admit. And *real*: a twin to the "old ladies'" calendar that Erin scorned. The buttercups shone as though painted with one thick dab of gold enamel, and the daisies were as white as new snow. Above the meadow the sky lay flat and blue, uncluttered by even a wisp of a mare's tail.

There's an old-fashioned poem that might have been written pre-cisely for this scene, a verse that would make the mature, sensitive poet cringe. It begins, "Buttercups and daisies, / Oh, the pretty flowers!" and continues with all the charming but saccharin sentiment of a Kate Greenaway illustration. Herrick might have written such lines. Or Thomas Campion, a poet of the 16th century. We appreciate the juve-nility of these lines only because they are very old, deciding that people must have been less complex, more credulous, in those times. Now we are realists, skeptics who'd be ashamed to be seen brushing away a sen-timental tear.

Nature isn't sentimental. Sentimentality is something that belongs to human emotions. We declare it in adults who react to experience in the simple, artless way of a child. The modern, serious artist doesn't copy nature; he interprets it according to the philosophy of his perception. It wouldn't do to paint a buttercup petal straight from the cadmium tube. Into that flower goes the whole life experience of the artist, his theory of art, his emotions, his aspirations. To paint what one sees as one sees it with the naked eye is sentimental and primitive, and no longer acceptable as a work of art. The personality of the artist gives depth and meaning to his work. And we who contemplate it feel, perhaps, a fuller, more perceptive appreciation.

But that doesn't make invalid the bright skies of an old-fashioned calendar. I wonder why we are ashamed to enjoy paintings of lilacs and landscapes that look exactly like lilacs and landscapes; or why we don't like to show if we are moved by rustic country scenes: cottages with roses round the door and little animals looking out at one with wistful, wondering eyes. I would rather be thought untidy and lazy, an ungrammatical writer who splits infinitives and puts apostrophes in all the wrong places, than sentimental.

Sentimentality doesn't belong in this century. Handkerchiefs are strictly for blowing noses, not for surreptitiously wiping away our foolish, tender tears.

THE RELUCTANT TURTLE

The turtle in the center of the highway may have been moving, but how can you tell with a turtle? I parked the car and rushed with virtuous haste to the rescue, fearing that she would be run over. When in doubt as to gender I tend to think female, and the name Ethel came to me as though I'd flipped a switch. She didn't seem too eager to be rescued, however, and hissed nastily in the back of the wagon, though I'd endeavored to make her comfortable with handfuls of grass from the roadside. "This is for your own good," I told Ethel as I drove her all the way to town and back. Later I deposited her, still hissing her protest, on the lake shore below our home, where, I was convinced, she would be a happy and grateful turtle.

Someone wiser than I asked, "How do you know where she wanted to go? Maybe she was on her way to her mate or had just finished laying her eggs and was hurrying back to the cool, refreshing water." I *didn't* know. It hadn't occurred to me that Ethel might have a mind of her own. Fired with do-gooder zeal, I'd rushed to do what I assumed was best for her.

This is the assumption under which many of the world's do-gooders operate: that they know what is most necessary for another's happiness. The well-intentioned offspring of an aging parent place Mother in an institution because her dress is sometimes back to front and the canary's droppings have spilled on the floor under its cage. They sit in their clean, comfortable kitchens discussing Mother's welfare over mid-morning coffee. "She may not like it at first, but she'll soon adjust. It will be good for her to be with people her own age with someone around to see that she's clean and tidy. She'll be happier in the long run." At the same time mother is at home lovingly cooing to Tweety-bird, rejoicing in her independence, unaware of jam stains on her collar and toast crumbs on the floor. She is confident, proud, and knows the priorities for survival.

"For your own good" is the definitive phrase which, accurately interpreted, means "for my own satisfaction." It isn't that do-gooders lack compassion. They may have an abundance of it. What they lack is empathy and the insight that comes from the earnest effort to see the situation from inside another's head. The proverbial boy scout who helps an old lady across the street hasn't stopped to inquire whether or not she wants to go. Intimidated by his formidable good intentions, she meekly toddles along.

"I know what is best for you," says the doting mother as she pushes her brawny son with gridiron ambitions toward the piano bench. What she means, could she only admit it, is that she knows what will bring gratification to her own heart. Having been denied the musical training for which she had always yearned, she wants desperately to believe that Junior has an artistic temperament, and she will sacrifice herself to the realization of this ideal. Junior is unhappy and grows up to be neither a Glenn Gould nor a Joe Namath but tries to comfort his unsatisfied aspirations by clerking in a sporting-goods store.

Most of us want to help others. With Christian love and missionary fervor we carry our scuttles of coal to Newcastle. But to "do good" effectively you must know what you're doing. Somehow, without prying too intimately, you have to think yourself into the shape of another's world with an imagination that is keen and intuitive. Human beings are like a bag of allsorts, similar on the outside but with fillings that are individual — chocolate, licorice, butterscotch. It is important that you understand the special ingredients of those you want to help. You have to know your turtle!

A ROOM WITH A VIEW

That picture of a dear, lonesome dog that hangs above my piano was obtained under false pretenses. Such odious tactics, which I have learned to employ in times of accentuating circumstances, achieved their goal, and I run no risk in admitting it now. The picture is a pencil drawing that evokes a mood of lonely yearning in its lights and shadow but mostly in the soft lines and profile of the black Labrador, who sits on a lawn behind a picket fence, head turned towards the road. It is a picture of waiting, that incredible patience that some creatures display as they watch for their particular human to come home.

This picture once hung in my daughter's bedroom in Fredericton, New Brunswick. For years Lorna has been buying the works of young Canadian artists of promise, not primarily as an investment but because her selections hold for her a strong personal appeal. My first glimpse of this work, by David McKay of New Brunswick, told me that it was something I must possess. I yearned for it as a dog yearns for the return of its human friend. I began by suggesting to Lorna that it would be a perfect birthday gift for a fond daughter to present to her mother on March 6th. The response was a flat "No."

"Well then," I persisted, "let me buy it from you."

There was no answer from that stony face as she glared out of the window.

"Lorna," I said, "I'll give you twice what you paid for it."

Her reaction was a kind of weary, long-suffering refusal, and I returned home pictureless but not defeated, as I contemplated my next attack.

It went like this and hit home on the first try: "I've been a senior citizen for a year now, which means I'm on the short end of it all. Sometimes I feel old, and I get depressed, wondering how much time I have left. That picture would give me so much pleasure in my few remaining years."

Leo, bless him, crated the masterpiece for me, and now it hangs in our living room on a lend-lease arrangement.

In this room the chesterfield lies against the north wall, and this is where I sit and write, my feet on the long, low coffee table between a Swedish crystal vase that Lorna bought for me with her first earned money and a solid glass horse, clear as a bubble, from the Corning Glass Museum in New York. I raise my eyes often as I write, seeing no familiar object, but only some inward scene of the past that my memory is exploring. But sometimes, I don't know at what signal, my attention is recalled to present reality, and I begin to notice those familiar possessions that live in this place and make it dear.

Most of them recall anecdotes, as does Lorna's dog, or else they are meaningful to me because of my regard for the giver. Andrew Wyeth's *Christina's World* hangs above the sideboard, the lame young woman sitting in a field, the circumference of her world drawn by the malady that warped her legs. Cecil gave that to me: my brother who left us early in September. The Wyeth was a favorite of his, and I gaze at it and remember my brother: how he read poetry to me and told me what clouds are made of and knew the names of the stars.

Nearby, inexorably marking the minutes of our lives, hangs the pendulum chime clock. I've written about that and my husband's exhaustive search for it. "I don't care about a chime. I want a clock that ticks." That ticking that I can hear when I'm alone in this room charms me as it did when I was a child, home from school before the others, sitting in the rocker in the afternoon shadows, the hush of my solitude described by the clock that Father made, there on the kitchen wall. I wandered about the rooms of that house when no one was there and with no sound save that from the eternal pendulum. Was there, then, some sort of comprehension in the silence, some mystery that I, moving stealthily through the doorway, could surprise? And it seemed to me that to discover that mystery would be to learn some deep cosmic truth denied the human spirit.

There on the sideboard stands the copper luster-ware pitcher from Poppy Crawford's Antiques, with sprigs of pussy willow and Chinese lanterns. And the brass spirit lamp I found at the Gutzeit estate at the time of its sale to the province. And Jack's mother's silver tea set and the brass silent butler that I wanted for so long, finally found for me by my sister at a garage sale.

A painting of deep personal value to me was done by Ruth Brooks, a fine, accomplished artist and friend. What I wanted, I told Ruth, was a young woman standing by a stream, gazing contemplatively into the water. Could she somehow suggest, without a dark shadow of gloom, a death wish in the woman's mind? More of a wistful wondering I wanted, not seeking so much to escape this life as a curiosity and a yearning for another where she could be alone and at peace. Ruth created the scene superbly. Faintly, so that it is discovered only by those who know, as I do, that it's there, floats the drowned image just under the stream's surface, pale and tranquil in her fulfilled desire.

And there's the Chinese print that Lily Crawford gave me, the silhouette of trees and rocks, stark yet delicate, like the crooked trail of a mite on wet sand. The artist was Yu Wan Chun, and Lily translated the characters to read:

Red leaves
And early autumn wind;
A small boat
And clear water

I've written before of Lily; niece of Madame Chiang Kai-shek. While visiting us one cool autumn day she fell in love with our dachshunds, Trudi and Treena, and, seeing them shiver as dachshunds do at the first nip in the blue October air, made them reversible corduroy coats, one red and one brown, which they enjoyed and wore proudly for the rest of their days.

This then, is my room with a view: four-dimensional, that fourth dimension enhancing the others, giving them a significance that is warm and profound. And that ambience interrupts my work, whatever it happens to be, to draw me into landscapes of the past.

THE DELIGHTFULLY WICKED MR. PUNCH

It wasn't until I was six or seven that Mother allowed me to walk on the avenue alone. Dangers lurked there, and there were rules I must observe if I wanted to arrive home safely: the ABCs for a child first venturing out alone. They were lessons that had little meaning for me: Never talk to strange men, don't accept candy from anyone, nor an invitation to go for a drive. Never wander down alleyways, nor cross the avenue. These rules didn't frustrate me. Germantown Avenue's attractions were exciting enough just for looking.

One needn't venture into Vernon Park to see what was going on there. The old, tall trees were far enough apart to allow a good view from the sidewalk. And there were open, grassy places with benches here and there. On almost any day there could be seen a straw-hatted man manipulating a dancing doll. Its wooden legs clacked together with the sound one could produce by running a stick along a board fence. Sometimes there was a three-piece German band whose contagious rhythm compelled the heart to beat along in time. There were people being walked by their dogs; students ambling along with arms full of books. Often there was a slobbering, red-faced fellow sprawled on a bench, talking to himself, and you knew that he was *drunk!* You stared fearfully for a moment, then hurried on by.

On fine summer days the fire station doors stood open and firemen sat about on metal folding chairs having a snack of a five cent Coke and a hot dog. Behind them, ready for instant take-off were the gleaming red fire trucks that compelled all traffic to halt as they sped over the cobblestones when an alarm sounded. I would pause there for a few minutes, shyly heeding their friendly teasing and threats to cut off one of my curls. They weren't *strange* men, were they? They were firemen! Surely it was all right to accept a lollipop when offered.

The most exciting sight I ever saw on Germantown Avenue was something I hesitated to describe to mother, though finally I couldn't resist blurting it out. I was on my way home, having come abreast of the Lyric Theater (a definite no-no), and about to turn the corner onto Wister

Street. Here I was astounded to see a wooden platform not far above my eye level, supported by a base that was hidden by a wrap-around canvas. I recognized it all as a stage, which was why I was reluctant to tell mother about it, for anything to do with theater was anathema among those of the "brethren assembly" to which I belonged.

A puppet play was in progress. I stood paralyzed with wonder, for how could those little dolls move about on their own? There was no visible puppeteer as with the step-dancing mannequin in Vernon Park. Where did the voices come from? The characters were costumed in vivid shades of red, yellow, and blue, and the most boisterous of them was a grotesque figure with a big, hooked nose that curved downward and almost touched his pointed chin.

This was, of course, a Punch and Judy show. The action was constant and crazy. Once over my first amazement I giggled along with the other spectators who had gathered round. There was Mr. Punch, dancing and jumping about; his wife Judy, a policeman, a doctor, etc. And the devil himself, whom I had no trouble identifying. I couldn't understand the dialog too well but I could see that Punch was the villain of the piece, who thwacked over the head any character who displeased him. The funniest scene was the final one where the devil tries to subdue Punch with a stick. That miserable blackguard pops up all over the stage but dodges in the nick of time when the devil's weapon strikes.

When the Punch and Judy show was first produced in English marionette theaters, the children would jump up and shout "There he is!" "There! — There!" The audience was often appealed to, as when Judy, not knowing a dog had eaten the sausages she'd left in Punch's care, turns to the engrossed children; "He did eat them, didn't he?" And the children shout back "No!" They respond with boos and cheers at appropriate times. The American audience with whom I watched the play that first time weren't familiar with this actor-spectator exchange. They simply laughed and applauded, moving away when a hat or box was offered for contributions.

I was reminded of the Punch and Judy play and this episode of my childhood as I watched the movie *My Left Foot*. A brief glimpse is given of the portable proscenium in a street scene of a town in Ireland. Suddenly the memory surfaced in my mind like Punch springing onto the stage from the property shelf below. I found myself wondering about Mr. Punch and his origins.

If I thought about him at all I'd have assumed that he was a char-
acter born and bred in Victorian England, a street show personality,
knock-about, and noisy. Certainly his popularity was at its peak in that
era. His origin, however, dates back to the 16th century in Naples, Italy,
where he was known as Pulcinello. There are several derivations given
for his name, the most probable being *pulcino*, a chicken, because of
Punch's beak, the way he walks, and his squawking voice.

The first reference to Punch in France is in 1649, where he was
known as Polichinelle. He had a hump then, and a prominent belly. The
French are silent about his Italian existence, preferring to believe that
he was born in their country, a personality of Gallic wit and humor; ego-
tistic, ruthless. It appears that Punch came to England not directly from
Italy but by way of France about the time of the Restoration. His name
Polichinelle was presently changed to the abbreviated British Punch, by
which title he is still known to all English-speaking peoples.

There was something else I'd forgotten about the Punch and Judy
show. And that was that I once played in a stage version while attending
boarding school in my teen years. How could I have forgotten that? I
was Judy and one of the lines I remember is one spoken when I grabbed
the stick with which Punch had been cudgeling me, and hit him back.
"And there's a little one for yourself," I yelled in glee. Also, there was
Punch's classic complaint: "I've got a bone in my leg and I can't walk."
The present younger generation probably never heard of it, but when I
was a child I thought it was hilariously funny.

There have been many versions of this puppet play, sometimes for
reasons of pleasing peoples of different cultures. Or to meet the
approval of those who believe that children should neither see nor hear
a drama in which right does not triumph. Here we have a story of mul-
tiple murders perpetrated by one Mr. Punch; there was his wife, Judy, a
constable, a doctor, a hangman, even his baby is thrown to its death out
the window. Finally Punch, after a feverish battle with the devil himself,
knocks that personage senseless to the floor. In triumph the ridiculous
victor dances an exuberant jig about the stage, singing in his high, raspy
voice "Bravo! Hooray! Satan is dead! And now we can all do as we like."

We might wonder how Punch gets away with all this and still plays
to an audience of young and old, who end up cheering his victory, and
his escape from punishment. It's because he makes us laugh. He does
"but poison in jest; no offense in the world." He expresses irresponsible

desires that may lie hidden in our subconscious minds, actions that we know we will never perform, and don't really want to. To see a wooden doll exulting in such abominable behavior must give us some measure of vicarious joy.

Even I, a six-year-old member of a sect rigidly moral and evangelistic, applauded the delightfully wicked Mr. Punch.

DACHSHUNDS IN THE GRASS

In my new backyard the grass is shining under the noon sun save where blossoming boughs of a young apple tree spill their shadows. Wild blue violets throughout the lawn are a bonus I hadn't reckoned on when we bought the house. I stand looking about me in wonder for it seems a small miracle that this is my home now. I am also looking about for another small miracle — a dachshund pup named Morgan. I call for him, worried that he may have made his way under the fence, for his breed are fine diggers. It's funny that I hadn't noticed before a narrow margin between the far side of the garage and the fence, overgrown with weeds and maple shoots. And this I discover now as I search for my little dog. There he is, seemingly contemplating this new world, sitting among a patch of creamy, long-stemmed white violets. Another bonus. Another blessed surprise.

They'd all heard me say it. "No more puppies," I told them firmly. Although I'd trained to fastidious habits in the past, four dachshund puppies over a period of thirty years, I no longer have the energy to cope with this beguiling bundle, comic and lovable, but so full of frenzied curiosity. "After awhile," I oft repeated in an effort to convince myself more than anyone. "After a while I might get an older dog from the Humane Society. I mean, one that's mature and sensible and likes to take dignified walks with its mistress."

So much for the resolutions of a weak-willed, gullible, just-on-the-edge-of old lady. Here he is, Morgan Drew, full of the aforementioned irrepressible curiosity up with which I was not prepared to put. My days at this stage are far from restful. Nor do I have my proper sleep. At first my rest was broken several times a night by Morgan's moving about and peering intently over the edge of the bed like a creature that has something urgent on its mind. I'd leap up, grab him and rush out the back door, at which, on six different occasions, I set off the burglar alarm. Dropping him onto the grass, I'd race back in to turn off the alarm, sometimes in my confusion, dropping the key and having to feel around for it on all fours because I didn't have my glasses on. This is not a happy experience for a stiff-jointed senior who had always thought of old age as a time of relaxed serenity.

Morgan is quiet through the night now. I lie with one ear open like a mother whose sleep is only as deep as her child's cry. I have been accused of spoiling my pets but this is not so. Although Morgan sleeps on my bed I refuse to allow him to get under the covers. I am most firm about this.

Dachshunds have their funny little ways. All breeds do, I suppose. But I'm thinking in terms of funny-peculiar. They are not brave animals. They can be fierce fighters when greatly provoked but mostly they prefer to withdraw, all the while trying to disguise their timidity with mild rumbles far down in the throat. Trudi and Treena, my dachshunds at Sandhurst, made a brave show of courage when accompanied by an able-bodied human. But watching from a window I have seen them head briskly for the house when threatened by anything bigger than a grasshopper. Swallows darting from their mud nest on the garage sent them running headlong for mother and safety.

At the time of the Millhaven breakout the Bath-Adolphustown area was under close surveillance. Driving to Napanee one day my car was searched four times. It was disconcerting to realize that a mild sort of person like myself could be as suspect as the next. At 1:00 a.m. when a helicopter with a searchlight went back and forth over our house I was home alone with only my two fearless watchdogs for protection. In spite of that I have to admit I was nervous. From the wall of my husband's basement office I took the shotgun hanging there. There was no ammunition for it, and it had never been loaded as long as we had it. Armed with this on the front porch with Trudi and Treena to bolster my courage, I thought we must look formidable enough that no convict would dare to accost us. I swung the gun slowly from side to side while the dogs raced back and forth across the lawn, excited by the glare of the searchlight and the noise of the motor. Finally, when I lowered arms and opened the door, the dogs were inside ahead of me. After the tumult, in the black of pre-dawn, when I could hear disturbing rustles and creaks from outside and wearily walked to the door to peek out, my German security force accompanied me, three feet behind.

A friend of a practical turn of mind asked me once, while admiring my pets, "They're fine-looking dogs. But what are they good for?"

What could I say? That they kept me from lying about and getting stiff and lazy, that they took my mind off myself so I didn't brood about my own problems? The real reason is, of course, that I keep them for love and affection. Not much of an answer to one who is concerned with practical values. But any dachshund person will understand.

YOGA AND ME

Thinking about breathing can be as disconcerting as thinking about thinking. The stewardess explains how to use the oxygen mask above my plane seat, and I begin to breathe erratically and wonder if I'm going to faint. This is why I never made such progress in the practise of yoga, for the control of the breath is common to all schools of this aspect of Hinduism. The attainment of physical and emotional self-control has always appealed to me, and at twelve years old I was leaping into an icy cold bath, even on winter mornings; then dressing in all the woolly garments I owned and jogging around the block at a time when *jog* was a simple, unembellished verb.

Ah, the ascetic life! A glorious ideal that I never attained. But I tried. I tried until well into maturity, at least that dubious maturity that I wear like a stiff, ill-fitting coat. There was the incident when Linda reported to her dad that Mother was standing on her head in the corner of the bedroom. He looked up from his paper to remark casually, "I'm not surprised. Does she have her gloves on her feet?" Well, you know how families are. They'd have taken me seriously had I been able to explain rationally what my purpose was. I was practising the yoga head stand, the *sirshasana* position.

My instruction book tells me that this is the most difficult of all the yoga poses: the "King of Asanas." Yet somehow I took to the upside-down posture like a diving duck. I reminded myself how much it benefited my system, as I noted carelessly the bits of fluff under the bed and discovered what had happened to Jack's missing shoehorn. If you find it monotonous to hold this pose it is suggested that you wiggle your legs. Some experts even assume an inverted lotus asana in this weird situation and swivel their hips about, a vision that stuns my imagination.

At one time I thought I had mastered the Lotus Seat, but learned later that it was an easier pose called the *padmasana* that I was holding. This I assumed in the apple orchard like Buddha under his fig tree. However, the complaints of an arthritic knee compelled me to give that up, and now my favorite position, the only one I can still do, is the Death

Pose or *savasana*. To achieve this you lie flat on your back, arms resting along your sides, and let yourself go slack like a sagging hammock. The only trouble with this is that I tend to fall asleep. When I tell someone that I didn't answer her phone call because I was practising the yoga savasana my explanation is accepted as though I had offered a half hour of Transcendental Meditation as an excuse: odd but legitimate.

What my youthful zeal was originally trying to achieve was a small holding in the suburbs of Nirvana, a hideaway so that life wouldn't hurt so much, for the adolescent spirit bruises so easily. In practising yoga procedures, so I read, I would learn the art of meditation, experience a greater awareness of the timeless Now, and finally drift into harmony with the "Is-ness of the Is." The hurts of life would then fall upon me as gently as dew upon the lotus blossom, and I would understand the profound meaning within the couplet

Sitting quietly, doing nothing,
Spring comes and the grass grows by itself.

Well, detachment may be the way for some. But for most of us life is for living, and I doubt if happiness is to be found by standing on one's head. Scarcely a thing of beauty and joy forever is the navel, that one should gaze upon it constantly for a lifetime. Buddha himself left his state of supreme detachment to acknowledge and teach his belief in man's responsibility to man. And Jesus lived and taught a life of involvement with and service to others. It's lovely to be alone and quiet and to commune with one's spirit in a place of peace. But we can't know how lovely unless we have come in out of the rain only for an hour's respite, not for a lifetime's retreat.

THE WHITE LEGHORN EXPERIMENT

Mother had fixed the henhouse roof, perched on the peak singing gospel hymns as she hammered away at the loose shingles. Such jobs of carpentry weren't exactly her forte, but Mother would tackle anything after a word of prayer and a transfusion of faith. This was a piece of property she had bought in upstate New York, a rambling farm house with a couple of outbuildings, a lovely broken-down stone wall by the orchard, and a yellow rose bush that we called "Joy." Mother and I lived here for two years, in a rather primitive fashion, it seemed to us, accustomed as we were to the many conveniences of city living.

It was here that we performed the White Leghorn experiment, brother Larry having purchased 60 of these pretty white birds, whose eggs we expected to gather every day and take to market, making ourselves a nice profit. Larry couldn't get away from his job in Philadelphia, but he had taken a correspondence course in chicken farming through Cornell University and felt qualified to direct his project by mail. "White Leghorns are good layers," he wrote. He didn't tell us anything about their temperaments.

Perhaps he didn't know that chickens of this breed are, or were, jittery creatures forever on the edge of a cackling conniption. Discussing our experience recently with a chicken farmer who knows all about leghorns, I learned that in the last 25 years or so this characteristic nervousness has been largely eliminated through selective breeding. In the process of genetic research the coolest chicks have been repeatedly mated until scientists have come up with a fowl of minimum flappability. But that was long after our acquaintance with them.

The pretty pullets were duly delivered and took up residency. Naturally we didn't expect them to begin laying immediately; they had emotional adjustments to make. Sometimes on an early visit to their quarters I would find a couple of eggs for our breakfast and would tell myself that a farmer's life was a good life. What could be fresher and sweeter than an egg warm from the nest?

But as time went on their output didn't increase greatly; not so much as to balance the cost of our input. They seemed to me to be unhappy and neurotically excited, though I talked to them in soft sympathetic tones, and crooned them lullabies. Not having an adequately enclosed run, they wandered into the house on several occasions, decided that they were in dangerous territory and tried to wander out again, but couldn't find the door.

We shooed them with brooms and dusters from the top of the piano, the cabinet, behind the couch. Finally they were ousted, and we cleaned up after them to a chorus of exhausted clucks from the henhouse at their traumatic experience. Although Mother had made their quarters rainproof, she had no ideas for weasel-proofing. The slim, sly animals slipped in under the walls, and many a night we heard the stark death squawk of a perishing pullet. Then the pip got them. We would bring the infected bird into the back kitchen, and there she would stand beside the grain barrel, looking like an apoplectic prima donna. We felt helpless before her extremity and suffered with her.

When their numbers had dwindled to a mere half dozen we thought we would finish them off, but neither of us could bear to deliberately extinguish that last sputtering spark of life within them. Besides, their meagre flesh would have made a scanty, not very palatable meal. So we waited for them to make their way at their own pace to happier pecking grounds. I was convinced that their gradual demise was the result of a collective death wish. They just didn't want to live any more.

Although my mother had great faith and enthusiasm it didn't necessarily follow that all her ventures were successful. The White Leghorn experiment was a failure, but far from a dismal one. Somehow it didn't' matter; we had had fun, and it had been a lively, enlightening experience. Certainly it didn't discourage Mother from the next project that Larry presented to us. Soon after, we had word that he had purchased, and was sending to us, 50 pairs of large bullfrogs which we could breed and raise and prepare for the lucrative frogs' legs market. We put on our high rubber boots, took up a carpenter's tape measure, and made our way to the mucky wet place by the edge of the wood. We had great expectations.

THE ADS THAT WERE

When Tom Hortman, the young man next door, gave me a pair of fancy garters, it was the first gift I'd ever had from a male outside my family. At seven or eight years old I was too young to be a flapper; nevertheless I wore them just below my knee over the ribbed stockings, and hoped they would show when I twirled about. For as long as I had those gaudy accessories I twirled around quite often. Tom worked in a garter factory, and that was big business then, turning out ladies' side and round garters of silk-frilled elastic with buckles and bows, as well as men's half-hose, advertised with the slogan "No sox appeal without Paris Garters."

Sex was a word that only a very bold little girl would utter, but we understood the pun all right. Sex appeal was something possessed by glamorous film stars, a term that was soon taken up by advertising firms. Magazines, newspapers and radio commercials had long been encouraging the human propensity to worry over the functions and malfunctions of our bodies, our desire for physical beauty and to possess the best, most modern version of all that technology had to offer. Now our advertisers wanted to convince us that *their* product was just what one needed to develop or enhance sex appeal.

You may remember the lady with the wistful eyes who was "often a bridesmaid but never a bride," because she didn't use Listerine mouthwash. Listerine is still going strong. The commercials have changed, but we still get that old Puritan message that anything that tastes or feels so unpleasant must be good for us. I doubt if the consumer believed that it increased one's chances of marriage.

That floating white soap, Ivory, advertised as 99-and-44/100 percent pure, kept the skin soft and was mild enough for baby. Its name was inspired by the "ivory palaces" in the forty-fifth Psalm and adopted by the young inventor Harley Procter. With the same trust we had in Listerine, we bathed in Lifebuoy, its strong antiseptic smell assuring us that it would indeed rid us of that dreaded B.O., a term that became a household word in the '20s. In the next decade we drove along the highway reading aloud, fast and furiously so as to get it all in, the Burma

Shave verses. We could sing as well about Barbasol: "No brush, no lather, no rub-in / Wet your razor, then begin." At that time we knew for sure that Bon Ami "hasn't scratched yet" and likely never would.

Tobacco has always been a favorite with the advertising agencies. Everyone knew what LS/MFT meant; it was printed on the Lucky Strike cigarette packages, and we heard it Sunday nights on The Jack Benny Show. Tense smokers were advised to "Be nonchalant. Light a Murad." Cremo cigars warned the fastidious against their rivals with the distasteful slogan "Spit is a nasty word but it's worse on the end of your cigar," while the discriminating smoker would "Walk a mile for a Camel."

Certain advertised products have stood the test of time, and today's consumer still looks for those brand names. "Mmm Good" aroused our appetite for Campbell's soup, and the Coca-Cola "Pause That Refreshes" is still familiar, though current commercials are more elaborate and crassly competitive. Phil Harris's radio show brought "Good Health to All from Rexall," while Charley McCarthy recommended Royal Pudding and Chase & Sanborn coffee. The margarine lady wasn't eating her bonnet then, but Fred Allen took us down Allen's Alley to the melodious message "Blue Bonnet Margarine with all three: / Flavor, Nutrition, Economy." Billie Jones and Ernie Hare were radio's "Interwoven Pair," and the little guy in the pillbox hat called over and over and over again for "PHIL-LIP MOR-ISSS." The Lord and Thomas advertising agency told us about "the soap that gets clothes RINSO WHITE and RINSO BRIGHT" on the fabulous Amos 'n' Andy show. Listening to those black-face comedians five nights a week became a national habit, a media feat unlikely ever to be duplicated by a sitcom show.

Assaulted by barrages of commercials from every side as we are today, copy that is often inane, odiously competitive, and *loud*, we may wistfully imagine a world where consumer products are introduced only over the store counter. But the old ads weren't so bad. Perhaps it's because time mellows the past, but it seems to me that they were more tuneful and amusing, more honest by way of naivete and sentimentality. Certainly they were less intrusive to our slower-paced way of life.

POT AU FEU

In 1976 I made a stew that took us a year to consume. Not that it was that large a pot; rather it was a kind of perpetual-motion thing, alternately boiled and refrigerated, to which I added vegetables and meat and various handy left-overs each time I served it. For a while it became a hobby in which my creative faculties were happily engaged in producing variations on a theme. A sad day it was when we ate the last morsel of carrot, and spooned the final drop of gravy. But, I told myself with a sigh as I scraped the sides of the empty pot, enough is enough.

I must confess that I didn't invent this continuing culinary treat. I only take credit (which may or may not have been given) for the innovations. Centuries ago French farm wives in the Medoc started their succulent stews with odd bits and pieces of animals that might elsewhere have been thrown to the livestock, added any vegetables in season and generous portions of the commoner wines and gave the concoction plenty of time to meditate and mellow. After the first meal this simple French cook leaves a bit in the pot to form the base for the next repast, on which occasion she adds to it any available, interesting edible that seems appropriate. This goes on for years and could become a legacy to her daughters. Who knows but that some of that original *lou pastis en pott* is still simmering away on the back of the stove in some kitchen in the south of France?

The very flexible recipe I used was suggested to me in the "Food For Thought" column of the old *National Observer*, an excellent publication that apparently hadn't the survival talents of its appetizing dishes. It began with salt pork and carrots, followed by layers of onions and figs, beef, seasonings and garlic, if you like. You ignite half a cup of brandy and pour it into the pot while it's flaming (which I found rather tricky), and cover all with red wine. This particular version goes into the oven, where all the vegetables and meat become friendly and sociable under the influence of the wine. One's family must be restrained from finishing it off so that there's a starter for the next time around. At its resurrection there may be added ham, lamb, sausage, turkey, more wine, and any other palatable bits that are lying about and want eating up. The wine will mellow and disguise.

My son-in-law, that mad philosophy professor who believes that the Earth is flat, discovered for himself the perennial potential of the simple stew. In an interview in a 1974 *Globe and Mail* he tells us that his Super Stew idea began with a desire to simplify the preparation of meals. One pot, he tells us, could last a lifetime, the method being that you put something in every time you take something out. "If you feel like a bit of fish, you simply buy a haddock or something, and toss it into the pot. The following day, or week, add whatever you like: beef, vegetables, clams, oxtail . . . and so on." He adds, bursting into laughter and slapping his knee, that his "kids wouldn't touch it."

The stew pot has always presented an interesting challenge to the imaginative cook, whether bubbling away in the kitchen of a stately mansion or on the back burner of a cold-water flat. The France of King Louis IX was said to be the age of stews, among other things. Tough meats were hashed or pounded into tenderness and mixed with wine and honey. Skylarks, quails, venison, ham, bacon were the nucleus for many a pot. I found a recipe for a Spanish stew served by Marie Therese to Louis XIV when they were married in 1660. It's called Olla Podrida: *Olla* indicating the pot and *Podrida* meaning, literally, "rotten," referring either to the smell of the rather high bacon or the seldom washed cooking vessel. The dish was a favorite of Sancho Panza's, who thought it "both wholesom and toothsom," and consisted of garbanzo beans, bacon, chicken, chorizo sausages, garlic, and pimentos.

The pot au feu can be a work of art, a collage to which all the family may want to contribute. Almost anything edible may be included, and almost anything can be made edible with long hours of TLC, as was proved by Charlie Chaplin with his high laced boot in an Arctic hut. Let your stew be a family project with each member naming an ingredient to be tossed into the pot. You may be surprised at some of their inspired suggestions.